RA

Rebellion!

Ireland in 1798

DANIEL GAHAN is one of the foremost historians on the events of 1798. He grew up in northern Co. Wexford, in an area alive with the lore of the Rebellion and the event captured his interest from an early age. He holds degrees from St Patrick's College, Maynooth, Loyola University of Chicago and the University of Kansas. He has written on the social history of Ireland in the eighteenth and nineteenth centuries; is author of *The People's Rising*, a study of Wexford in 1798; and has also featured in a television documentary series on the subject. He teaches history at the University of Evansville, Indiana, USA, where he lives with his wife and two children.

REBELLION!

Ireland in 1798

Incorporating a Yearbook of
1798 Bicentennial Commemorative Events

DANIEL J. GAHAN

THE O'BRIEN PRESS
DUBLIN

First published 1997 by The O'Brien Press Ltd.,
20 Victoria Road, Rathgar, Dublin 6, Ireland.
Tel. +353 1 4923333; Fax. +353 1 4922777
e-mail: books@obrien.ie
website: http://www.obrien.ie

ISBN 0-862785-413

This book is a joint publication with Comóradh '98

British Library Cataloguing-in-Publication Data
Gahan, Daniel
Rebellion!: Ireland in 1798
1. Ireland – History – Rebellion of 1798
2. I.Title
3. 941.5'07

1 2 3 4 5 6 7 8 9 10
97 98 99 00 01 02 03 04 05 06

The O'Brien Press receives assistance from
The Arts Council/An Chomhairle Ealaíon

ACKNOWLEDGEMENTS
The publishers wish to thank the following for their kind permission to reproduce illustrative material in this book. All possible care has been taken to trace copyright holders. If any errors or omissions have been made please notify the publishers and corrections will be made in subsequent editions: Kilmainham Jail pages 1, 6, 15, 16, 17, 18, 21, 23, 25, 26, 30, 32, 33, 34, 41, 47, 71, 95, 101, 107, 108, 114, 117, 120, 121, 125, 130; National Library of Ireland page 38, 39, 49, 51, 54, 58, 62, 64, 66, 74, 79, 85, 87, 91, 93, 98; Wexford County Library Map Collection page 46.

Typesetting, editing, layout, design: The O'Brien Press Ltd
Maps: Ronan Hayes
Cover separations: Lithoset Ltd
Printing: MPG Books Ltd

Contents

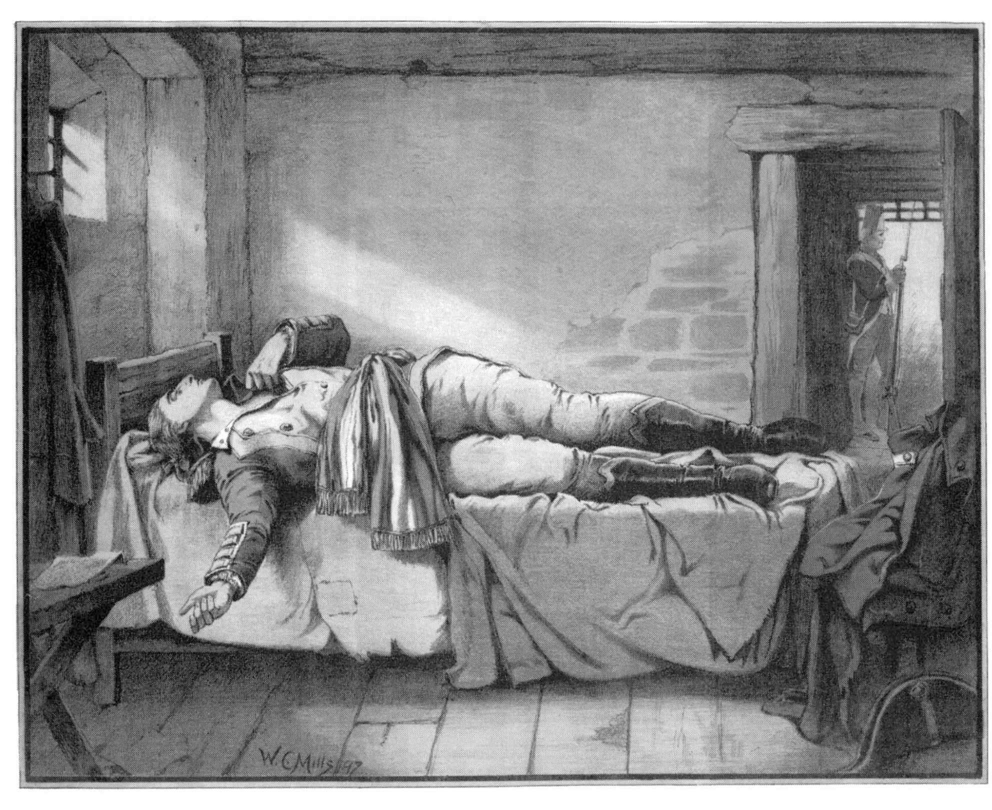
W.C Mills 97

Foreword

The 1790s was one of the most critical decades in modern European history. *Rebellion! Ireland in 1798* sets out to discuss the Rising in 1798 as of some, if limited, importance in the history of that broader context, as well as of significant importance in Irish and British history. The author Daniel Gahan traces the development of the United Irishmen and the revolutionary movement which developed in the 1790s, with French assistance, and dispels the myth that '98 was a localised rebellion.

This book explores the ideas and ideals that inspired the republicanism and non-sectarianism of the United Irishmen, the nascent nationalism of the Irish peasants and tenant farmers and the remarkable degree to which Catholics and Presbyterians found common cause in a rebellion against an oppressive and unjust government. The strategy and tactics of the opposing forces are explained and the battles and encounters of the war described. In addition, Daniel Gahan has a keen eye for the strengths and foibles of those individuals central to the Rebellion.

Above all, however, this is an account of the leading part that the men of Wexford played in the Rising once they became involved and of the terrible price the county and its people paid for their participation. Two hundred years after the Rebellion, the ideas that inspired men like Bagenal Harvey, Edward Fitzgerald, 'the bould Father Murphy' and many others are still valid for their descendants.

As one of the foremost historians on the events of 1798, Daniel Gahan has long been acclaimed in Ireland and the US as an excellent writer. *The People's Rising*, his previous work on the Rebellion of 1798, stimulated a huge interest in the period. Here, he brings the rebellion to life in vivid detail, sparing the reader none of the military tactics or atrocities which occurred on both sides, nor does he seek a revisionist interpretation of history.

Rebellion! Ireland in 1798 is also the official book of the National 1798 Visitor Centre in Enniscorthy, Co. Wexford. It contains a yearbook with a comprehensive listing of the 1798 bicentennial commemorative events and a chronology of the historical events of the Rising. This work, then, ranks as a important contribution to our complete understanding of the events surrounding the '98 Rebellion, the legacy of which still haunts us today.

Bernard Browne
Comóradh '98
Enniscorthy

Counties in which Significant Actions Occurred
Tone and Hardy
Tandy
Humbert
DONEGAL
DERRY
(LONDONDERRY)
ANTRIM
ULSTER
TYRONE
FERMANAGH
ARMAGH
DOWN
MONAGHAN
SLIGO
MAYO
LEITRIM
CAVAN
LOUTH
ROSCOMMON
LONGFORD
CONNACHT
MEATH
WESTMEATH
GALWAY
OFFALY
(King's County)
DUBLIN
KILDARE
LAOIS
(Queen's County)
WICKLOW
CLARE
LEINSTER
CARLOW
KILKENNY
LIMERICK
TIPPERARY
WEXFORD
MUNSTER
WATERFORD
KERRY
CORK
1796 Expedition (Hoche)
Counties in which significant actions occurred

CHAPTER 1

THE RISE OF THE PEOPLE

1760 to 1789

On the evening of 23 May 1798 one of the most destructive rebellions in all of Irish history broke out in the counties immediately around Dublin. Within a few days it had spread to most of the south-eastern part of the country, centred around Wexford, and within two weeks to the predominantly Presbyterian counties of Antrim and Down. In this early phase, the rebellion did not extend outside the provinces of Leinster and Ulster. Towards the end of the summer there was a separate, though connected, uprising in Co. Mayo, sparked by a landing of French troops and soon to spread into neighbouring counties. By the time the 1798 Rebellion or 'Rising' was over, tens of thousands of people had been killed and millions of pounds-worth of property destroyed. It also left behind a legacy of bitterness that, two centuries later, still afflicts Ireland.

The ideas that led men and women to hilltops in Ireland in the summer of 1798, weapons in hand, can be traced back for generations, even centuries. They had their roots at the beginnings of western culture, springing in part from fundamental Judeo-Christian insights about the nature of humanity and the sanctity of every human being as well as the Old and New Testaments' emphasis on social justice. They had their origins too in Greek philosophy and Roman law and in a medieval West which, though dominated by kings, still would not countenance the unchecked power that men call despotism and which persisted in lands far to the east.

For the most part, however, the ideas for which the men of Wexford and other parts of Ireland fought in '98 remained half-buried for centuries in mankind's consciousness. The Renaissance in Italy in the fourteenth to sixteenth centuries began to reorient European peoples to a vision of man as a dignified creature, even though a fallen one. The German and Swiss Protestant Reformers of the early 1500s would assert the right to stand by what they believed to be true and challenge anyone's right to force them to do otherwise. John Calvin, the father of Presbyterianism, contended that to rebel against an ungodly king was the right of any good Christian.

A relevant – if distant in time – prelude to the 1798 Rebellion in Ireland was to be found in the Civil War or 'Great Rebellion' in England from 1642 to 1652. The parallels are not direct but that war stemmed from motives similar to that which drove the men of '98 to war – Puritan rejection of the Stuart kings' claim to rule by divine right. Even Cromwell, who was to lay waste the greater part of Ireland, was impelled by Calvinist fervour for just and godly government (at least in his own country), the same fervour that drove tens of thousands of his fellow Puritans to establish self-governing communities on the other side of the Atlantic. In England, however, the supremacy of parliament was not to be established until the 'Glorious Rebellion' of 1688.

It was the eighteenth-century 'Enlightenment', however, which was the proximate cause of the upheavals of the 1790s in Ireland and elsewhere. Locke, Kant, Voltaire and others were to emphasise the primacy of reason and science over traditional prejudices and unscientific beliefs, judging what is rational as good and what is not as the opposite. Rousseau, while rejecting rationalism, believed in the natural goodness of man and saw good government as being created by free individuals voluntarily entrusting part of their freedom to the state for the common good. Their ideas were to form the basis of modern democracy and provided the inspiration for the revolutions and republicanism of the later decades of the eighteenth century.

The '98 Rebellion, therefore, was more than a chapter in the story of Irish nationalism. It had a long pedigree, culminating in the enormous intellectual and political upheaval that shook the entire European world over a period of eighty years or so between the 1760s and the 1840s, the effects of which are still being felt. Certainly, nationalism played a part in that upheaval and so it is legitimate enough to see 1798 in that context. But it was also about the rise of the modern concept of 'the people' and of the sanctity of the people's will, of their sovereignty. The underlying ideas were long in developing and by the 1840s they had much maturing still to do. But the set of political values that we choose to call 'democracy' today emerged out of this period in America and in various parts of Europe. Over the next several generations young men and women in many countries would dedicate their energies and their lives to this ideal.

For the generation that saw the '98 Rising, that ideal was still a long way from being formulated, let alone achieved. The Europe of the second half of the eighteenth century was a curious mix of societies. The eastern lands of Russia, Poland, Hungary and Germany across the Elbe formed a vast zone of serfdom. Outside the few main cities with their aristocrats and artisans, the mass of the people worked on huge estates, tens of thousands of acres in many cases, where they were little better than slaves. In this feudal society, they belonged to their lord and master, were obliged to work the land they lived on for him and him alone and could neither leave nor marry without his consent. The only governors were the lord in his castle and the monarch in his palace. This was a despotic world without juries, without parliaments, without freedom in even the most basic sense.

Western Europe, Ireland included, was a different world. Here the land was worked by peasant farmers who, in a few cases, owned it outright. Mostly, however, the great majority of farmers were tenants on smaller estates – 5,000 acres or less – than those in the east. Their life was never easy and peasant farmers everywhere had to worry about the weather and prices, facing the possibility of ruin and even starvation if either failed them. They could, of course, walk away from their holdings if they wished but only the life of the pauper faced them if they did. There was still a degree of fluidity in these Western societies with a vibrant and growing network of towns offering opportunities unavailable in the east.

There were, however, stresses and strains in Western Europe that would reach breaking point in the closing decades of the century. Political power and its exercise was the exclusive or nearly exclusive preserve of the landed élites though dispersed to one degree or another among many hands in all parts of the West. Even in the so-called 'absolute monarchies' of Austria, France, Spain and Portugal, there was provision for an assembly of the nobles to advise and direct the king in especially critical situations. At the other end of the spectrum, there were self-governing peasant communities in the Swiss mountains that functioned in many respects as democratic republics and in the Netherlands there were seven small provinces, most the size of an average Irish county, which were self-governing merchant-dominated 'republics'.

In the British Isles and in the British colonies in North America a system somewhere between the near-republicanism of the Netherlands and the absolute monarchy of France prevailed. Almost all of George III's dominions had representative assemblies of some kind when he acceded to the throne in 1760. Great Britain itself had a parliament, as did Ireland, and the colonies in America had various sorts of assemblies: only the Caribbean island colonies were ruled by appointed governors. In reality, however, the King and the aristocracy of England monopolised political power. By manipulating the corrupt parliamentary electoral system, they so dominated parliament that it was not an independent body at all; moreover, the parliament of Ireland was subordinate to that of Britain and the assemblies of North America were, at least in theory, subordinate to Westminster too. Throughout Western Europe, only property-holders were entitled to vote: the accepted wisdom of the time was that government was rightfully the preserve of those who by blood or worldly success were worthy of the privilege of participating, directly or indirectly, in the function of governance.

Similar privileges were associated with membership of Europe's many established churches. In the Orthodox lands of the east, the Catholic lands of the south, the Lutheran lands of Scandinavia and Germany and in the Anglican lands of King George, men and women were expected to profess the state-sanctioned religions or be subjected to political and civil disabilities. In only a handful of places, among them the Netherlands and some of the British North American colonies, was there anything approaching religious tolerance, though here and there, because of the tortuous history of the Reformation, minorities followed a different religion from that of their ruler. In the Balkans, Christians were ruled by Muslims, Lutherans in the Baltic by Orthodox Russians and Catholic Ireland by a Protestant monarch.

Ireland of the mid-eighteenth century, therefore, presented many of the typical features of Western European society of the day. Its parliament was elected by the propertied and overwhelmingly Protestant minority. Parliament had very little real power and the landlords, who administered law throughout the kingdom, like landlords in every other corner of Europe, were effectively the king's agents in the countryside. The lot of the Irish countryman and his family was typical enough too of that in most of the rest of Western Europe. He paid rent, in cash or kind (or even labour) to a landowner who held a modest estate, a thousand acres or so in most cases. Most landlords would certainly have considered themselves gentlemen though few were genuine aristocrats. Port towns and market towns brought the countryman and his family face to face with the commercial world of the merchant and trader on market days and fair days. Up to about 1760 they might still not conduct business exclusively through cash but they were used to handling money and had come to think of the world in commercial terms. There were exceptions to this of course: along the west coast and in the uplands the change to a money economy had not yet taken place and there were landless or near-landless labourers everywhere. In general terms, though, the Irish countryside had long since been caught up in the commercial economy of the Atlantic world and had begun to devote most of its land area to producing either directly for that world or for the Irish towns that traded with it.

There were some unusual features about late eighteenth-century Ireland too. Catholics and Presbyterians, whose churches were discriminated against, made up some six-sevenths of the island's population but still constituted a minority of King George's subjects. Unlike the French landlord class, the Irish landed elite had acquired its land through conquest and confiscation and this ensured a continuing deep sense of injury among the dispossessed Irish Catholics. Ireland was unusual too because its large Presbyterian population, amounting to about one-sixth of the total, was concentrated in the eastern parts of Ulster. Most of them were tenant farmers, occupying small but prosperous farms and also involved in the weaving trade. They were part of a larger Presbyterian world in the

Lowlands of Scotland and in the many communities in the foothills and mountain valleys of the back country of North America. Industrious and prosperous despite their limited resources, they had the same spirit of independence and distrust of over-powerful kings as Calvinists elsewhere although, like the Catholics, they were excluded from political life by the ruling Anglican elite.

This Europe of remote and poor rural regions and thriving urban centres, of absolute monarchies and republics, had long since begun to question the whole idea of rule by a privileged few. In Ireland the legitimacy of English rule had been opposed for generations because it was alien and because it was Protestant. The legitimacy of the landed elite had been resisted, many times by force of arms, because they were perceived as robbers and upstarts. Many of the hard questions that would be asked in the closing decades of the century were also being formulated in Ireland. The forces that would bring the end-of-century storms from Sicily to Norway and from the Appalachians to the Urals were being mustered. Ireland would quickly find herself caught up in them too.

CHAPTER 2

THE STORM BREAKS

1760 to 1794

The storm began to gather in the 1760s. The key year was 1763 in England a radical journalist named John Wilkes was elected to the Commons, was refused entry and was re-elected again and again. He championed parliamentary reform and supported the cause of the American colonists against the King. The cry of 'Wilkes and Liberty' echoed throughout the English-speaking world for a whole generation. In 1763, too, King George initiated punitive taxes and duties on his North American colonies and triggered the American Revolution. There were similar upheavals on the Continent. Peasants in Scandinavia and the poor of Paris rioted for cheaper food; in Geneva, merchants conducted a bloodless revolt for the right to fill half the seats on the city council. In Ireland, there were riots in Munster, south Leinster and east Ulster against the enclosure of common lands and against church tithes. In Munster and Leinster, Catholic peasants formed 'The Whiteboys', a secret organisation which operated mostly at night, conducting a relentless peasant resistance to rack-rents and evictions that would last well into the following century. In Ulster, the 'Hearts of Steel' emerged as an active terrorist force in the Presbyterian heartland, demanding security of tenure and other agrarian concessions. The conviction was growing that the poor and marginalised had some basic rights and that resort to violence to achieve those rights was legitimate.

The 1770s saw more direct challenges to the structures of power. In 1771 a coup in Sweden brought the aristocracy into power and considerably weakened the king. In 1773, a peasant army of 20,000 men swept over a vast region of southern Russia before the Czar's troops crushed them brutally. Two years later in Bohemia, a 15,000-strong peasant army, revolting against forced labour, marched on Prague and intimidated the Hapsburg monarchy into granting them concessions. The 1776 American Revolution was directed against a particular king and a particular aristocracy but it also presented itself to the world as a struggle for universal liberty and equality and for republicanism as a viable way to organise a modern state. It triumphed in the field by 1781 and two years later George III recognised the new republic.

Theobald Wolfe Tone: founder of the United Irishmen, in a French uniform.

Ireland was bound to feel the effects of at least some of these developments. In 1778, the Dublin parliament passed a law permitting Catholics to lease land for 999 years, thus making their tenure a little more secure. Four years later another law permitted them to buy their land outright. The Protestant class was beginning to relinquish its monopoly on the ownership of land, renting direct to tenants and cutting out the land agents and middlemen, signalling for some that the old order in Ireland was eventually going to unravel. Demands for parliamentary reform and for genuine Irish independence also began to emerge, mainly among a minority of Protestant parliamentarians. A 'Patriot Party', led by Henry Grattan and inspired by the American colonists' success, demanded greater autonomy for the Dublin parliament. It won a measure of home rule but only until the 1800 Act of Union abolished the parliament in Dublin and appeared to put an end to all talk of independence.

As the decade of the 1780s was ending, Europe's power structures had begun to make some concessions to the forces building up underneath. But they misjudged the strength of those forces, resisting the pressures as long as they could and when the dam finally broke they were taken by surprise.

Lord Charlemont: commander of the Volunteers and a leading Irish Protestant liberal in the 1780s and 1790s.

The French Revolution of 1789 which was to breach the dam so rudely was the turning point in the history of the modern world. The Declaration of the Rights of Man, promulgated by the Constituent Assembly in August of that year, became the call to rebellion for those who resented privilege all over Europe. Even the calendar was changed to begin again with Year 1 in September 1792, an indication that the French revolutionaries considered the declaration of the French Republic a more important date than the birth of Christ.

In Ireland, reaction to the developments in France was at first generally favourable but later atrocities turned many, particularly the conservative Protestant landed élite and the Catholic Church, against it. In Ulster, however, the Presbyterians supported the ideals of the revolution and Bastille Day was celebrated more cheerfully in Belfast than in any other part of Britain or Ireland. Here, reformers such as Joseph Pollock, Dr William Drennan, a Presbyterian proponent of radical reform, and William Todd Jones preached equal rights for all religions, hinting that only in a fully independent Ireland could this be achieved. In 1791 a group of mostly Presbyterian radicals in Belfast, including William Tennent, Samuel Neilson and Henry Joy McCracken, established the Society of United Irishmen hoping to unite Protestant, Catholic and Dissenter in the struggle. They dedicated themselves to seeking the reduction of Ireland's dependence on Britain, the reform of parliament and the end of religious discrimination. Though it was not initially a part of their programme, they turned increasingly to the pursuit of outright independence. They were joined by a group of Protestants based in Dublin, including Theobald Wolfe Tone, Thomas Russell,

William McNevin: one of the prominent Catholic members of the Leinster United Irish movement. He was arrested before the Rising and later pardoned as part of the agreement with prominent prisoners. He then went to America and built a distinguished career as a doctor in New York.

James Napper Tandy, John and Henry Sheares, Archibald Hamilton Rowan and Thomas Addis Emmet. William Drennan and several Catholic merchants and professionals, including Dr William McNevin and Richard McCormick, also joined.

Leading Catholic laymen and some bishops became more vocal too, the younger of them demanding the right to vote and to sit in parliament. However the older, more conservative elements, Anglicans especially, prominent among whom was a Co. Wexford landlord, George Ogle, counselled caution. In spite of Ogle's spirited denunciations the bill giving Catholics the vote was passed in April 1793, three months after Louis XVI of France went to the guillotine. In Irish terms it was almost as great a revolution as that of 1789. Now Catholics with specified property qualifications could vote in county and borough elections, though still only for Protestants. Still the pace of reform was too slow for the increasingly strident and competing radical voices demanding it. Catholics were still not allowed to sit in parliament or to hold offices of state. The emergence of more politicised and more radical fronts among all religious persuasions alarmed the government which in 1793 disbanded the Volunteers, originally formed to

Fanciful sketch reflecting late nineteenth-century nationalist idealism: it shows Wolfe Tone, Thomas Russell and Samuel Neilson swearing to work for the ideals of the United Irishmen at McArts Fort, on Cave Hill near Belfast.

defend Ireland against foreign invasion during the American War of Independence and which had become increasingly vocal in its demands for full Irish independence. Many of the Volunteers, especially in Ulster, promptly transferred their allegiance to the United Irishmen.

In February 1793 the British government declared war on the revolutionary regime in Paris: from then on support for France amounted to aiding the enemy and, therefore, treason. The Irish authorities took the usual steps to prepare for war, the most important of these being the decision to create a much enlarged militia, with a regiment or two from every county, functioning essentially as the national army. Outside east Ulster, the rank-and-file was composed mainly of Catholics, officered by Protestants. Arming Catholics could not have been contemplated a generation earlier and indicated that the authorities felt assured that, because of the franchise reform, the Irish could be trusted to support the king. Despite some riots against conscription, including one in Co. Wexford where scores of protesters were shot, the draft went ahead and in a year the militia was raised and deployed, each regiment being assigned to a county other than its own. In the meantime, the government, with the open support of the Protestant

Ascendancy and with at least the tacit support of the Catholic bishops, moved against groups suspected of sympathising with the French, among them the Society of United Irishmen which was banned. Some chose to withdraw from the Society altogether; most became more radicalised and adopted an outright republican agenda.

In the meantime, the French Revolution had passed into a new phase. The more moderate Girondin party had finally defeated the Jacobins, who had been responsible for the mass executions of the aristocracy during the Terror, while the Revolution was being consolidated inside France. Moreover, France had introduced mass conscription and by the end of 1794 had driven back the armies of the alliance powers and had invaded and taken control of much of the Austrian Netherlands (modern Belgium). With hundred of thousands of conscripts at its disposal, the Paris regime was now poised to carry the fight to its opponents for the first time and to begin the work of spreading the Revolution.

CHAPTER 3

THE UNITED IRISHMEN AND THEIR PLAN

1794 to 1797

In 1794 the Jacobin government in Paris began to explore the possibility of invading Ireland as part of the grander strategy of knocking England out of the alliance against France. Early in the year an Anglican clergyman, Rev William Jackson, who had lived in France for a long time and was a supporter of the Revolution, was sent to Ireland to assess the reception such an invasion might have. By this stage, the United Irishmen had been banned by the government and become an underground organisation, still only a few hundred strong and mainly confined to the middle-class of the towns, especially Dublin and Belfast. Jackson contacted the leaders, who included Wolfe Tone, and, having established that they were unquestionably dedicated to the idea of separatism and republicanism, foresaw an alliance with revolutionary France as part of their strategy.

That autumn, however, Jackson was arrested in Ireland and put on trial as a spy (he committed suicide in the dock) and Wolfe Tone surrendered. The following June, Tone went into temporary exile in the United States but kept his ambition for an Irish republican revolution very much intact and remained in contact with the other leaders of the movement at home.

During 1795 a series of events transpired that would give the United Irishmen a whole new appeal. Two developments in particular were critical: in January Earl Fitzwilliam, a member of the more liberal Whig faction in England, became Viceroy of Ireland; and that summer the Orange Order was founded. Catholics anticipated that Fitzwilliam would use his influence to complete the passing of the Catholic Emancipation bill. Fitzwilliam did wage a brief war of sorts against the Irish Protestant Ascendancy but they managed to have him recalled to England the following month. To the immense disappointment of Catholics, a petition to the King to reinstate Fitzwilliam was rejected. The effect was to alienate a great many more Catholics, especially the more well-to-do and politically ambitious, and turn them more than ever to separatist – even

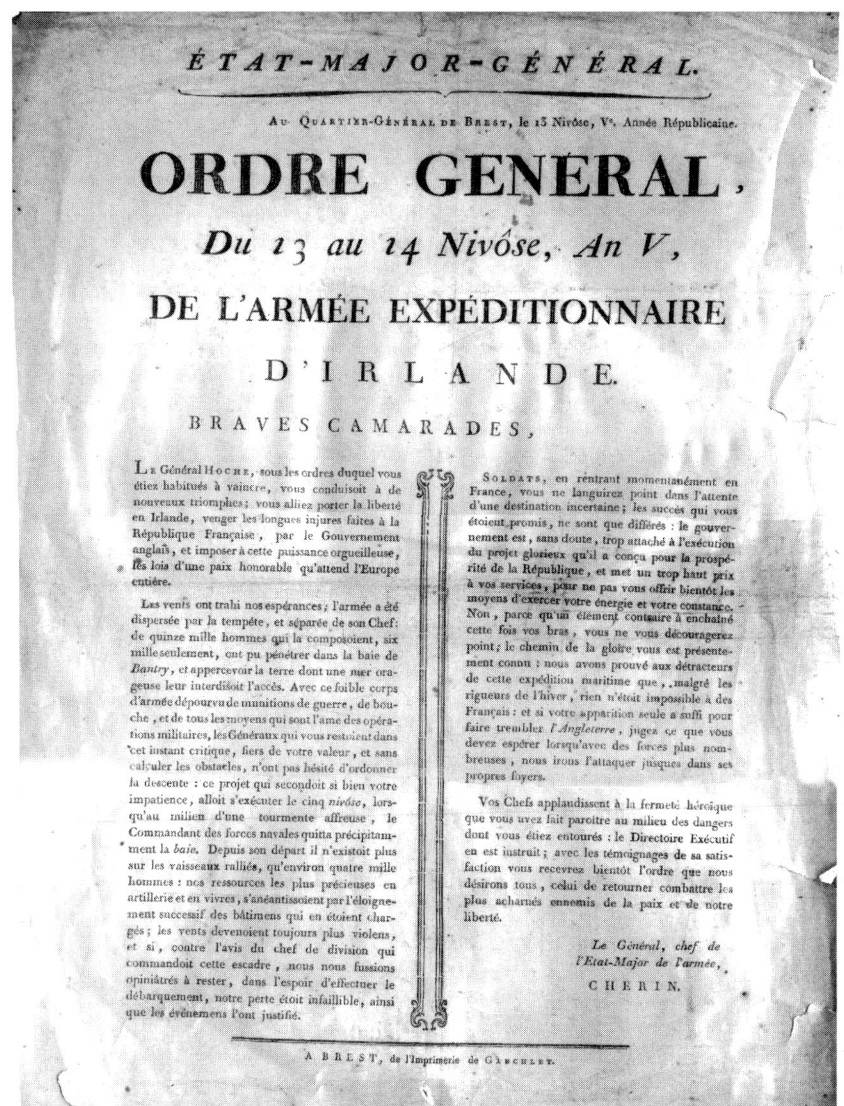

ÉTAT-MAJOR-GÉNÉRAL.

AU QUARTIER-GÉNÉRAL DE BREST, le 13 Nivôse, V^e. Année Républicaine.

ORDRE GENERAL,

Du 13 au 14 Nivôse, An V,

DE L'ARMÉE EXPÉDITIONNAIRE D'IRLANDE.

BRAVES CAMARADES,

LE Général HOCHE, sous les ordres duquel vous étiez habitués à vaincre, vous conduisoit à de nouveaux triomphes; vous alliez porter la liberté en Irlande, venger les longues injures faites à la République Française, par le Gouvernement anglais, et imposer à cette puissance orgueilleuse, les lois d'une paix honorable qu'attend l'Europe entière.

Les vents ont trahi nos espérances; l'armée a été dispersée par la tempête, et séparée de son Chef: de quinze mille hommes qui la composoient, six mille seulement, ont pu pénétrer dans la baie de *Bantry*, et appercevoir la terre dont une mer orageuse leur interdisoit l'accès. Avec ce foible corps d'armée dépourvu de munitions de guerre, de bouche, et de tous les moyens qui sont l'ame des opérations militaires, les Généraux qui vous restoient dans cet instant critique, fiers de votre valeur, et sans calculer les obstacles, n'ont pas hésité d'ordonner la descente : ce projet qui secondoit si bien votre impatience, alloit s'exécuter le cinq *nivôse*, lorsqu'au milieu d'une tourmente affreuse, le Commandant des forces navales quitta précipitamment la *baie*. Depuis son départ il n'existoit plus sur les vaisseaux ralliés, qu'environ quatre mille hommes : nos ressources les plus précieuses en artillerie et en vivres, s'anéantissoient par l'éloignement successif des bâtimens qui en étoient chargés; les vents devenoient toujours plus violens, et si, contre l'avis du chef de division qui commandoit cette escadre, nous nous fussions opiniâtrés à rester, dans l'espoir d'effectuer le débarquement, notre perte étoit infaillible, ainsi que les évènemens l'ont justifié.

SOLDATS, en rentrant momentanément en France, vous ne languirez point dans l'attente d'une destination incertaine; les succès qui vous étoient promis, ne sont que différés : le gouvernement est, sans doute, trop attaché à l'exécution du projet glorieux qu'il a conçu pour la prospérité de la République, et met un trop haut prix à vos services, pour ne pas vous offrir bientôt les moyens d'exercer votre énergie et votre constance. Non, parce qu'un élément contraire a enchaîné cette fois vos bras, vous ne vous découragerez point; le chemin de la gloire vous est présentement connu : nous avons prouvé aux détracteurs de cette expédition maritime que, malgré les rigueurs de l'hiver, rien n'étoit impossible à des Français : et si votre apparition seule a suffi pour faire trembler *l'Angleterre*, jugez ce que vous devez espérer lorsqu'avec des forces plus nombreuses, nous irons l'attaquer jusques dans ses propres foyers.

Vos Chefs applaudissent à la fermeté héroïque que vous avez fait paroître au milieu des dangers dont vous étiez entourés : le Directoire Exécutif en est instruit; avec les témoignages de sa satisfaction vous recevrez bientôt l'ordre que nous désirons tous, celui de retourner combattre les plus acharnés ennemis de la paix et de notre liberté.

Le Général, chef de l'Etat-Major de l'armée,

CHERIN.

A BREST, de l'Imprimerie de GAUCHLET.

Declaration issued to French troops after the failure of the Bantry Bay expedition, assuring them that their efforts, thwarted by the weather, had not been in vain and that the struggle (implicity, in Ireland) was to be carried on.

revolutionary – ideas, in spite of the fact that the French regime was clearly no friend to Catholicism. This revolutionary turn among Irish Catholics can be explained only by their disillusionment with their own government and their, perhaps naive, assumption that the anti-Catholic excesses of France would not occur in an Irish republic.

The second development took place in the south Ulster heartland of sectarian hatred. There, in the summer, the Orange Boys were re-organised into a more structured secret society known as the Orange Order and given the blessing of local landlords. Both before and shortly after this, the running sectarian war in Armagh spread south as Catholic refugees settled in northern parts of Leinster and Connaught, bringing their secret society, the Defenders, with them. The Orange/Defender blood feud belonged in many ways to a world utterly alien to that of the United Irish struggle against monarchy and religious intolerance. But it became part of the public debate over the Catholic question that was so much on the minds of the politically active and politically aware in the country at large. Eventually, all three struggles (the Orange/Defender struggle, the Emancipationist/Ascendancy struggle and the republican/monarchist struggle) would begin to feed off one other.

Events on the Continent in 1795 made the rising tensions along these Irish fault-lines all the more serious. Up to the end of 1794 the French revolutionary armies had been fighting for survival and foreign troops, British and Austrian included, were occupying various positions around the perimeter of the country. Only along the frontier with the Austrian Netherlands (Belgium) had the French actually driven the invaders back and themselves invaded a foreign territory. On Christmas Eve 1794 they followed up these advances with an invasion of Holland. By the end of January they had captured Amsterdam and by May they had concluded a treaty with the new 'Batavian Republic' as the old Dutch Republic was now called. By the end of 1795, the French armies had also finally crushed most of the internal uprisings that had been hampering them and had signed peace treaties with Prussia and Spain. The tide was turning in France's favour now and in at least two places, Belgium (which she annexed directly in October) and Holland, she made it clear that she was serious about expanding the Revolution. To William Pitt, the British Prime Minister, and to the Ascendancy faction in Ireland these were disturbing developments and they would make the situation in Ireland all the more disconcerting.

In 1796 the French tide continued to swell. In the spring Napoleon Bonaparte was given charge of a military campaign in Italy and by the summer he had turned most of that country into a French satellite. He invaded the Papal States in June and in October established republics in a large part of northern Italy. Freedom of worship had been restored in France in February of 1795,

Lord Edward Fitzgerald: veteran of the American War, admirer of the French Revolution and commander-in-chief of the United Irishmen until his capture on 19 May 1798.

allowing the Catholic Church to attempt to rebuild, but Napoleon's conduct in Italy showed both that France was still an enemy to the Catholic Church and that she was determined to continue to expand republicanism where she could. The other major powers on the Continent, Prussia, Spain and Austria, seemed unable to prevent this and by the autumn Britain was actually sending out feelers for peace.

During the course of 1796, the United Irishmen movement grew rapidly. At the beginning of the year the Society was still modest in size but by year end it had achieved remarkable success among the Presbyterian tenantry and townsmen of eastern Ulster and had thousands, perhaps even tens of thousands, of sworn members, many of them armed with home-made pikes or guns left over from the days of the Volunteers. The movement was now drifting towards revolution and a large part of the Presbyterian population was involved, perhaps because they had been republicans in sympathy for a long time (i.e. since the days of the American Revolution) and were attracted to the idea of establishing republicanism either in Ireland itself or in the British Isles in general.

The movement also acquired a broad appeal among the Catholic population of Leinster, especially northern Leinster, the very area in which the openly sectarian Defenders were winning a lot of recruits at the same time. Unquestionably there was a connection between the two organisations here and many Defenders seem to have joined the United Irishmen over the course of the year, attracted less by their non-sectarian agenda than by their anti-government and separatist positions. It was unlikely that the Defenders would have had much sympathy for republicanism, especially since that was the gospel of a French regime which, despite the granting of freedom of worship, was still practically at war with the Catholic Church.

The Defender/Orange Order struggle, however, continued unabated and by the end of the year the Defender movement was well established in the northern half of Leinster and much of northern and eastern Connaught; the Orange Order in the meantime had spread southwards too although not quite as rapidly or as far. As the United Irishmen became a mass movement, a case could be made that the organisation had a different character in the Catholic heartland of Leinster from that in eastern Ulster. The fact remains, however, that the founding members and most of the leaders, regardless of whether they were Catholic, Presbyterian or Anglican, were still attracted to the non-sectarian and republican dream that had inspired them from the start. In the meantime, the Catholic population in general remained frustrated by the failure of the government to grant political emancipation. Earl Camden was now the Viceroy and, while he was not necessarily a captive of the Ascendancy faction, he was nonetheless perceived as being no friend to emancipation.

By 1796 the Irish government was aware that things were getting out of control and took steps to maintain its grip on the country. In February, the Insurrection Act allowed magistrates to impose martial law in regions they declared to be in a state of rebellion and brought in the death penalty for the administration of illegal oaths. In November, *habeas corpus* was suspended throughout the country. The militia, now well established and creating local tensions of its own, was to be the chief instrument for the enforcement of these new laws but the government had to authorise the formation of part-time yeomanry corps, to be raised by landlords and magistrates out of their own or their neighbours' tenantries, to supplement them.

Significant too in the evolution of the situation was the fact that two members of the Irish parliament, Arthur O'Connor and Lord Edward Fitzgerald, joined the United Irishmen in 1796. Fitzgerald had fought against the American revolutionaries, had been in France in the early 1790s and had expressed strong support for the Revolution and yet was a member of one of Ireland's oldest aristocratic families. His background, his ideological position and his military experience made him a vital asset.

In the meantime, the most important developments of 1796 took place in

The Buck's Head where United Irishman Thomas Russell ('The Man from God Know's Where') stayed. It is typical of the large inns in Ulster and other parts of Ireland during this period.

Paris. Wolfe Tone had arrived there from America in February and, with tremendous energy and considerable skill, as well as his share of deception, convinced the French government to dispatch General Lazare Hoche to Ireland with 15,000 men at the end of the year. It was a bold and risky move on the part of France but with Napoleon triumphant in Italy, with Prussia and Spain cowed and with Austria and Britain showing signs of weakness, it was obviously one way to end the war should it succeed.

Hoche sailed from Brest on 15 December and the fleet arrived at Bantry Bay a few days before Christmas. But disastrous weather destroyed the expedition: twenty of the thirty-five ships returned home, fifteen made it into the bay only to be storm-bound there for a week while only 400 troops landed and they were wiped out by the local yeomanry. The Irish government, however, had shown itself to be totally unprepared for a foreign invasion and when the danger had clearly passed most people, regardless of their viewpoint, believed that the French would have succeeded had they landed in force. The episode took place so quickly that the United Irishmen had no chance to mobilise and so did not reveal their real strength and membership. The Bantry Bay episode, however, gave the authorities a salutary warning and they decided to crush what they rightly regarded as a fifth column for France before a second French expedition could be launched. Ordered

Letter from Henry Joy McCracken in Kilmainham Gaol, dated 27 June 1797, and addressed to his sisters. It reads:

Dr Sisters, When I was removed to this part of the Jail. I thought that I would have a better opportunity of writting[sic], that is I would have more leisure, the reverse is the case, if you wish for a true picture of the inside of a Jail read the 2nd Chap, 2nd Vol, of Caleb Williams, from being confined with such a variety of Characters & all sorts of crimes charged on them, it makes a sort of amusement observing the different turns of mind, in the appartments allotted to us six northerns, we have got two very respectable men from the Rock on treasonable charges – Since our removal my linen has made a great decline, however I have still 4 Shirts – It is expensive to live here plundered by Turn Keys etc – & still more so when confined with others who cannot support themselves nor yet be left to themselves. You may easy see that I wish for some money: but not much. I received the two guinea notes. & two that John paid for me which is all that I have got to support myself & some others since the 10th May – I hate money it makes one melancholy to think about it, & has entirely prevented me writting this time – we are all well get the use of a yard all day & play ball from morn to night – Will is writting by the same oppty. God bless you all, H N J McCracken to disarm the United Irishmen in Ulster, General Gerard Lake declared martial law over a wide area and proceeded with terrible brutality to use torture and executions to gain his objective. By the autumn of 1797, the United Irishmen had been badly damaged and Lake's pre-emptive strike may have been a key factor in their ultimate failure.

For the time being, however, the movement had lost ground in one region only to gain it in another. As Lake was unleashing havoc on Presbyterian Ulster in 1797, United Irish recruiting agents began to make extraordinary progress in southern Leinster and eastern Munster, especially among Catholics. Even more moderate Catholics, disappointed at the failure of the emancipation movement, joined up, despite the opposition of the bishops to secret societies in general and their hostility to the goals of the United Irishmen. Throughout the country, United Irishmen propaganda, in the form of ballads, pamphlets and, above all, Thomas Paine's *The Rights of Man*, his famous defence of the French Revolution against Edmund Burke's attacks, drove home the message that change was desirable and could be achieved only through revolution. By the end of 1797, even as far south as Wexford, the United Irishmen were numerous enough to lead a group of magistrates to proclaim a section of the northern part of the county to be in a state of rebellion.

On the Continent, meanwhile, the position of revolutionary France became even stronger. Almost all of northern Italy fell into French hands in the spring of 1797 and when Pope Pius VI signed a humiliating treaty with Bonaparte in February, all of Italy, with the exception of Naples, became effectively a French possession. In addition, Britain had made more peace overtures in September, only to have them rejected, and had to fight off a Dutch challenge to her naval supremacy. That same month the Austrian government agreed to the Treaty of Campo Formio, whereby she recognised France's gains, both in the Low Countries and in Italy. As the winter of 1797/8 approached, therefore, Britain found herself utterly alone, at war with both France and Spain and facing the imminent threat of a French invasion force, of which Napoleon had been appointed commander. The government in Ireland now set out feverishly to eliminate the United Irishmen. Henry Grattan, long regarded as the chief spokesman for moderation in the Dublin parliament, withdrew with his followers though he still refused to support the United Irishmen, leaving the extremists on the government side with a free rein.

CHAPTER 4

BRIGHT MAY MEADOWS

1 January to 23 May 1798

At the beginning of 1798, Napoleon Bonaparte was the most powerful man in France, even though the government was nominally in the hands of a five-man Directory. His military victories in Italy and the death of Hoche (by natural causes) late the previous year had left Bonaparte almost alone at the pinnacle of power within France, with his only serious enemy abroad now being Britain. For the first two months of the year he fixed his gaze northwards. He consulted at length with the United Irishmen delegates, Wolfe Tone and Edward Lewins, and appeared to accept their assurances that an expedition to Ireland would be a military success. He directed invasion preparations along the northern coast of France and at the same time tightened his grip on France's northernmost satellite in Amsterdam.

In March, however, Bonaparte changed direction. Since the autumn of 1797 Swiss 'patriots', wanting to create a unified republic of Switzerland (in place of the very loose confederation that existed up to then), were active in Paris and their leader, Peter Ochs of Basle, was a major competitor with Tone for the ear of Bonaparte. He and his supporters concluded that a general uprising of the Swiss people against entrenched interests would be needed to reform Switzerland and remodel its government along French lines. The French had already attacked Mulhouse, a city-state near the French border, and followed this up by the invasion and annexation of Geneva in March. Bitter civil war now broke out throughout Switzerland between pro- and anti-French elements. The Catholic districts were overwhelmingly anti-French and some of the worst bloodshed took place here when a French army was sent into the mountains by Bonaparte in April and May to crush these Catholic communities with great brutality, shooting hundreds of country people and their priest leaders. In late March the Helvetic Republic (the new name for Switzerland) was proclaimed, giving France yet another satellite republic adjacent to its frontiers.

In Italy, there was yet another significant development. Pope Pius VI was by now practically a prisoner of the French government and to seal the triumph of republicanism over the Catholic Church the French declared the city of Rome and the region immediately around it to be the 'Roman Republic', forcing the Pope to flee the city. This step, coming in the same month as French soldiers mowed down Swiss Catholics in the Alpine Valleys, further demonstrated to the conservative forces of Western and Central Europe what was in store for traditional institutions, the Catholic Church included, should republicanism triumph everywhere.

Bonaparte now decided to drop his plans to invade England and/or Ireland in favour of leading an expedition across the Mediterranean to Egypt. This decision ensured that the United Irishmen were to be strung along for months on end with vague promises of a French expedition which would inevitably be much smaller than originally envisioned and was unlikely to depart anytime soon.

In Ireland itself the United Irishmen were continuing to expand. In spite of the setbacks in Presbyterian Ulster the previous summer, they now had a membership of around 100,000, perhaps even more, and a well-honed organisational structure. Where it had been established, each parish had a cell and each barony was run by a committee, elected from those parishes; the baronial committees in turn elected a county committee and they in their turn elected delegates to a provincial directory. In theory there was to be a National Directory too but, in reality, since the organised baronies and counties were almost all in either Ulster or Leinster, the Leinster Directory functioned *de facto* as the National Directory. Even so, not all Leinster counties had representatives as the year opened; the handful of counties immediately around Dublin seemed to be the strongest at this point (i.e. Dublin county itself, Meath, Kildare and Wicklow), and these, along with Antrim and Down in Ulster, still represented the geographical centre of the movement.

At the beginning of the year the Leinster Directory was dominated by a handful of men led by the two MPs, Lord Edward Fitzgerald and Arthur O'Connor, but prominent also were Thomas Addis Emmet and William McNevin. As they waited patiently for reports from France and as Bonaparte built up his forces along the channel, a split developed in the United Irishmen leadership over whether or not they should await a French landing before rising. O'Connor and Fitzgerald pushed for an immediate rebellion with or without French help while most of the Directory objected. By February the arguments became so embittered that O'Connor left the country (he was arrested in England at the end of that month and imprisoned in the Tower) and, in spite of Lord Edward's presence, this enabled Emmet and the 'French strategy' faction to take control. This in turn ensured that, from the month of March onwards, the Directory was urging the organisation to remain as clandestine as possible, to minimise violence including raids for arms, to cut down on drunkenness and in

Arthur O'Connor: member of Irish parliament who joined the United Irishmen in 1796. He was arrested in England in 1798 (before the Rising) on his way to France but acquitted of charges. He fled to France and remained there for the rest of his life.

general to do everything to avoid precipitating a government crackdown before a French landing could take place.

As the months passed, however, it became increasingly hard to do this. For one thing, the British government and its Viceroy in Dublin, Earl Camden, tried hard to destroy what they correctly regarded as a pro-French fifth column in their midst. They were aware from Lake's campaign against the Ulster Presbyterians of the previous summer that the movement was serious and well armed. They were also aware, through their extensive spy network of the movement's plans to link up with a French expedition. In late February and early March, Leonard McNally, a prominent member of the movement in Dublin, began to feed the authorities information about contacts with France and the extent of the movement. About the same time, Thomas Reynolds, a Kildareman and a member of the Leinster Directory, turned informer and provided further details about its plans.

The movement itself played into the hands of the government. The departure of Arthur O'Connor removed one of the most violently outspoken figures from the leadership (his newspaper *The Press* had advocated revolution openly) and this gave the Emmet faction control of the Leinster Directory. Emmet thought a successful link-up with a French landing required the movement to avoid attracting the notice of the authorities in the meantime. However, armed bands, mostly of Defenders, embarked on a series of night-time attacks on the houses of the gentry, apparently to acquire arms. Most of the attacks took place in eastern Munster and the midland counties but they suggested to Camden that a general revolutionary uprising was clearly being planned. Many of the gentry barricaded themselves into their houses, giving the impression in some areas that a war was already on.

The government then decided to move against the United Irishmen, hoping to arrest the core of its leadership and thereby decapitate it. On 12 March they raided a meeting of the Leinster Directory at the Dublin house of a woollen merchant named Oliver Bond. In that raid and in others conducted elsewhere in the city the same day, they captured sixteen leading members of the movement. Lord Edward Fitzgerald escaped and went into hiding, as did most other prominent members still at large, now that they realised that the government had a means of identifying them. In the next few weeks, a new Directory emerged, this time dominated by John and Henry Sheares, who believed in pushing ahead without French help, and Samuel Neilson, one of the founding members of the movement. With Lord Edward Fitzgerald in hiding, the movement was left effectively in the hands of the Sheares brothers.

In the country at large, too, the movement recovered from the arrests. In spite of its apparently centralised nature, the United Irishmen was really a confederation of local organisations. Each barony was led by a colonel and almost all of these were still at large and unidentified by the government at the end of the month, while each county had as its nominal leader the adjutant-general, chosen from among the colonels and few of these were known to the government either at the end of March. While the arrests at Oliver Bond's house were a severe blow, therefore, the movement continued to win recruits in the last half of March and preparations for armed uprising continued throughout Leinster, eastern Munster and even eastern Ulster.

Within the government in the meantime, a fierce struggle had developed between a group of hard-liners headed by John Foster, the Speaker, who wanted to crack down on the United Irishmen immediately, and a more moderate group which counselled moving more cautiously. On 30 March the Foster group won the struggle and convinced the government to proclaim the entire country to be in a state of rebellion. This was, in effect, the beginning of an all-out war against the United Irishmen. The various regiments of regular soldiers, along with the militia and the yeomanry, were recruited to fight this war under General Sir Ralph Abercromby, a Scotsman.

Abercromby's forces, numbering about 40,000, were widely scattered

John Sheares: one of the Sheares brothers, both early members of the United Irishmen and among the movement's key figures between March and May 1798. John was arrested before the outbreak of fighting, and executed during the rising.

throughout the country and he was appalled at their unpreparedness and indiscipline. Faced with the knowledge that the French might invade Ireland at any time, he had to decide whether to concentrate his forces in one place immediately to stop the French from marching on Dublin or to try to destroy the United Irishmen quickly before worrying about the French. Forced by circumstances to adopt the latter approach, he issued ultimatums in various parts of the country, starting with counties Tipperary, Queen's County (now Laois), King's County (now Offaly) and Kildare, demanding the surrender of all arms by a certain date, failing which the local inhabitants would be obliged to billet his troops free. By thus punishing everyone in a particular region Abercromby hoped to force the local United Irishmen into the open.

However, he had alienated many hard-liners in the Irish establishment, partly by his criticism of their excesses in hunting down suspects. Before he had a proper chance to apply his free quarters policy there was a successful move to oust him and he left the country on 23 April, to be replaced as commander-in-chief by General Lake, who had conducted the brutal disarming campaign in Ulster the previous year. Instead of applying Abercromby's free quarters approach, Lake

Henry Sheares: brother of John, and also executed during the Rising.

preferred a more direct assault against the United Irishmen. Within a few weeks, he had launched in Tipperary, Queen's County and King's County a campaign of judicial torture, house burning and mass arrests, especially of blacksmiths who were assumed to have made pikes and, therefore, to know the names of many United Irishmen. The campaign was carried on into Kildare and Wicklow and by the third week of May thousands of arms had been surrendered to the military. Of the counties that had strong United Irishmen support, only Meath, Carlow and Wexford had not yet been given ultimatums for the surrender of arms.

Lake's campaign threatened to eliminate a large part of the movement's army and when Lord Edward Fitzgerald received a message from Paris on 17 May that the French forces would not get to Ireland until August, the Leinster Directory realised that if they were to continue to wait for the French there was every chance that they might have no army with which to meet them. At an emergency meeting that day, the leaders decided to start a rebellion without French help the following week (Wednesday, 23 May). Two days later the

Samuel Neilson: founding member of the United Irishmen who became a central figure in the last days before the Rising but had a serious drinking problem and was arrested on the eve of the outbreak.

government captured Lord Edward as he was preparing to go to Kildare to lead the Rising from there. The following day, acting on information from spies, they tracked down and arrested the Sheares brothers. This blow to the head of the movement, along with the blows Lake had delivered at its body over the previous three weeks, almost brought it to its knees.

Only Samuel Neilson, a broken man at this point in his life, was left to lead the movement and even he was arrested on the afternoon of the twenty-third. The result was that a rump of the Dublin leadership drummed up a plan to conduct a bold and dramatic rebellion: units within the city were to seize members of the government as well as several prominent public buildings and military barracks; at the same time rebel units in Meath, Kildare and Wicklow would move in on the city and seal it off. Units in counties outside this inner ring would then mobilise and do their part in tying down government forces stationed there. For weeks there had been little regular communication with these outlying areas, Antrim and Down included, but the plan was probably as good as could be pulled together at a time when French help could no longer be expected and when the revolutionary movement was faced with the prospect of being arrested out of existence if it did not strike soon. In spite of the disasters of the previous weeks when twilight came on 23 May, thousands of United Irishmen mobilised in the rural districts around Dublin. Two days earlier, however, government forces had initiated the disarming of Dublin itself and had learned that something was planned for that night. Mobilising the entire garrison of around 4,000 men, they took possession of key points throughout the city and even though the rebel mobilisation went remarkably well in the outlying areas they were unable to deliver the crucial blow in Dublin itself. The most critical part of the desperate plan, the seizure of the government and the main public buildings, never took place and any chance there was for an Irish revolution succeeding without the aid of French troops was now gone. The rebels who had mobilised in villages and at crossroads throughout the countryside of southern Meath, northern Kildare and northern Wicklow did not know this. Nor did members of the United Irishmen in counties like Antrim and Down or Carlow and Wexford, who were located at either extreme of the chain of eastern counties where the movement had taken hold but where even the details of the plan itself were obscured in the alarm and confusion that had reigned for the past month. Outside of this eastern tier of counties, in places like Munster and Connaught, the United Irishmen were even less certain about what was to take place. Co. Mayo was probably typical of these areas and here the United Irishmen, while anxious to act, remained too weak and too apprehensive to make a move.

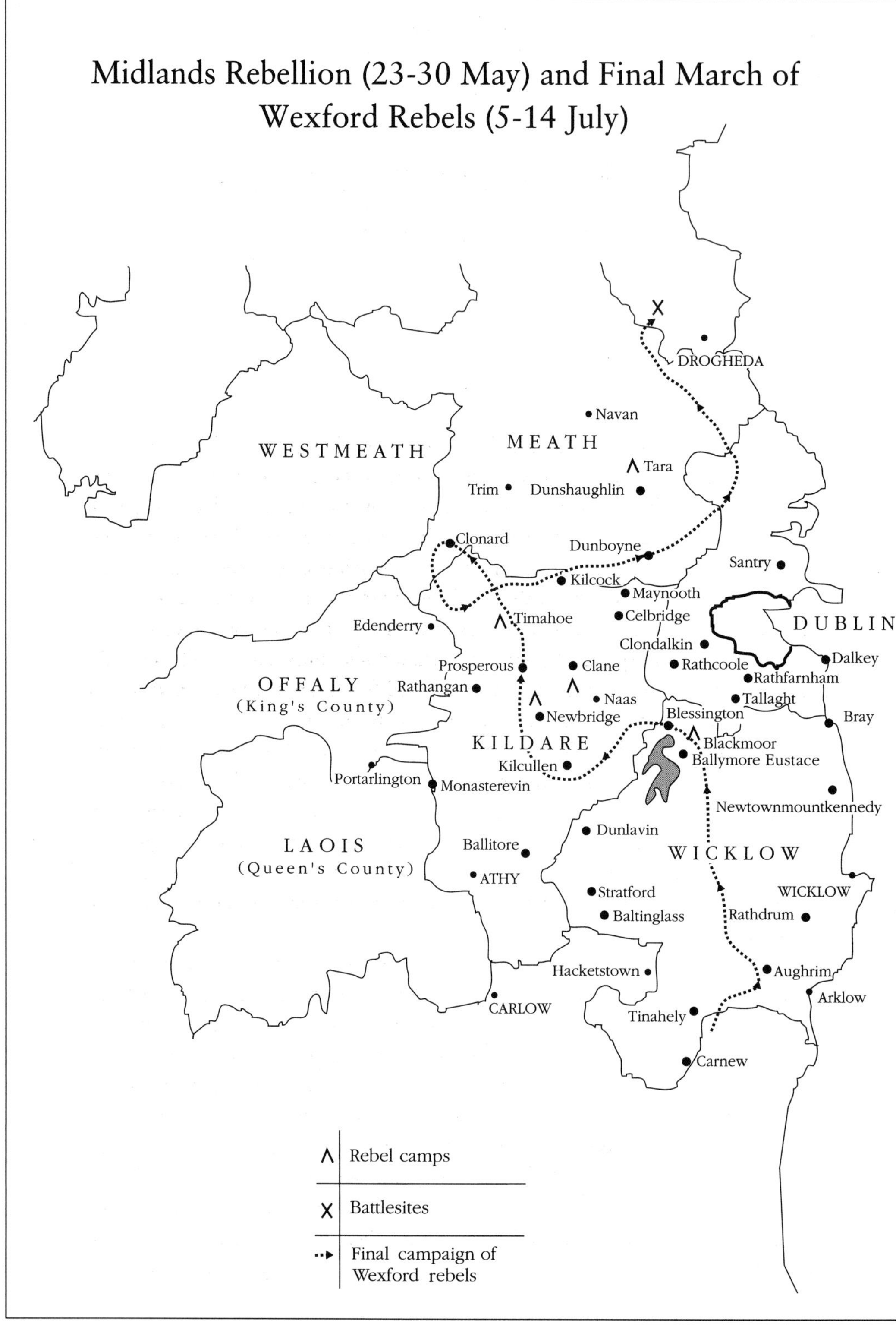

Midlands Rebellion (23-30 May) and Final March of Wexford Rebels (5-14 July)
DROGHEDA
Navan
MEATH
WESTMEATH
Tara
Trim
Dunshaughlin
Clonard
Dunboyne
Santry
Kilcock
Maynooth
Timahoe
Celbridge
DUBLIN
Edenderry
Clondalkin
Dalkey
Prosperous
Clane
Rathcoole
Rathfarnham
OFFALY
(King's County)
Rathangan
Naas
Tallaght
Newbridge
Blessington
Bray
KILDARE
Blackmoor
Ballymore Eustace
Kilcullen
Portarlington
Monasterevin
Newtownmountkennedy
Dunlavin
LAOIS
(Queen's County)
Ballitore
WICKLOW
ATHY
Stratford
WICKLOW
Baltinglass
Rathdrum
Hacketstown
Aughrim
Arklow
CARLOW
Tinahely
Carnew
Rebel camps
Battlesites
Final campaign of Wexford rebels

CHAPTER 5

THE RISING OF THE MOON

24 to 27 May 1798

The first few days of the rebellion were bound to be critical for the United Irishmen. They were operating without their leaders and in a situation confusing for all involved, those on the government side included. In spite of many disadvantages, particularly the fact that the rebellion never even materialised in Dublin itself, the United Irishmen achieved considerable success in their first four days. However, their failures were also significant and after only four days the situation was already very much in the government's favour.

The first twenty-four hours saw tremendous confusion on all sides. The rebel plan, hastily devised though it was, called for columns of insurgents on the outskirts of Dublin to stop the five overnight mail coaches from the capital to the main provincial towns. This would be a signal to units throughout the country that it was time to rise. As it turned out, only two of the coaches were actually stopped: the coach going to the North was attacked around midnight near Santry and set alight; the Cork coach was not stopped near the city, as it was supposed to have been, but got almost as far as Naas in Co. Kildare before being set upon by another rebel column; in this case the passengers were dragged out onto the road and killed.

Despite the failure to stop the other coaches and the general confusion, the rebels managed to mobilise thousands of men under cover of darkness, between twilight on the twenty-third and dawn on the twenty-fourth, in a broad sweep of country from north Co. Dublin, through the southern part of Meath and northwest Kildare to north Wicklow. Rebel columns several hundred strong attacked villages and small towns where government troops were stationed to capture arms. In Prosperous, a small mill town in north Kildare, they surprised and disarmed a garrison of around sixty men, killing most of them. In Old Kilcullen, ten miles further south, another column assembled in a churchyard and repulsed several assaults by a cavalry unit sent at them from Kilcullen village itself. In Meath the rebels took possession of the village of Dunboyne unopposed.

'Plan of a Travelling Gallows': The campaign against the United Irishmen before the Rising, as represented by nationalists in the nineteenth century.

'Captn. Swayne Pitch Capping the People of Prosperous': the nationalist representation of the campaign against the United Irishmen in Kildare before the Rising.

Apart from this handful of successes, most of the rebel columns formed that night failed in their immediate objective. Hundreds of men attacked the garrison in the village of Clane, Co. Kildare, and were repulsed with heavy losses. At Naas, a more heavily garrisoned town, a rebel column led by Michael Reynolds, the leading United Irishman still at large in Kildare, attacked around dawn and was driven off with the loss of several hundred men. Even at Kilcullen, a mile from Old Kilcullen, where the rebel column had earlier defeated a cavalry unit, that same column was driven from the field later in the morning by General Sir Ralph Dundas, commander of the Midland District.

In north and west Wicklow and in north and south Dublin the story was similar. Rebel bands gathered at Rathcoole, Tallaght, Rathfarnham and Dalkey during the night but efforts to take Clondalkin and other villages south of the city failed. Small and badly-equipped bands of Wicklow rebels were beaten off by the garrisons at Dunlavin, Baltinglass, Ballymore and Stratford. That afternoon, to intimidate soldiers who might be sympathetic to the rebels, the commander of the Dunlavin garrison had thirty of his own men who were Catholics taken out onto the village green and shot. This was only one of a number of dreadful massacres that day and it discouraged rebel efforts to drum up support in this part of Wicklow. Meanwhile, the rebel columns in north Co. Dublin disintegrated into a number of small bands by afternoon and the rebel grip on this district became very tenuous.

Inside the capital, the Viceroy, Earl Camden, could be sure only that the rebellion had been crushed inside Dublin and that it had broken out in the counties immediately around the city; he knew little about what was going on in places like Munster or Ulster. He decided to hold the city with his garrison, now swelled to six thousand men, yeomen included, and to take no chances on an offensive until reinforcements arrived from England. General Dundas, his commander in Kildare, adopted a similar approach and concentrated all his forces in Naas, Athy and Monasterevin. Taking quick advantage of the situation, the rebels continued to mobilise during the day and by nightfall had taken possession of almost every remaining town and village of significance in Co. Kildare.

Friday, 25 May 1798

On the second day of the rebellion, Friday 25 May, the bodies of rebels killed the previous day before were put on display in the Castle yard in Dublin and several suspected rebels were hanged on Carlisle Bridge. Among them was Dr John Esmonde, an officer in the Sallins yeomanry in north Kildare and brother of Sir Thomas Esmonde, a leading Wexford Catholic landlord. Meantime, the rebels consolidated their grip on those parts of Kildare and Meath they had captured the day before. They formed large camps on the Hill of Tara in Meath, at three strategic points in Kildare – Timahoe bog in the north of the county, Knockallen Hill near Kilcullen and Gibbet Rath near Newbridge, overlooking the road to Cork, and on the summit of Blackmoor Hill in north Wicklow, from which they could observe the countryside for miles around. The situation in all of these camps must have been chaotic. The colonels in command of the various barony regiments with the captains and rank-and-file members of the movement were present. What they lacked was a commander-in-chief for the entire United Irishmen forces; this was to have been Lord Edward Fitzgerald's role but he was in gaol. And so, a half-dozen or so men, all claiming to be colonels, found themselves in charge of each camp without any clear plan. They could not resume the attack on Dublin without help from the movement elsewhere nor could they disperse to their homes as they were now known to the government and could expect only to be caught and executed. They decided to wait on events in the rest of the country. They were to be disappointed.

'98 insurgent: probably an accurate portrayal of what a pikeman would have looked like at the outset of the fighting. By its end the Wexford rebels, in particular, were in a dishevelled state.

That day, the fighting spread to other areas. Several small rebel columns unsuccessfully attacked the villages of Lucan, Leixlip and Kilcock along the road to Galway and remained cut off from each other at the end of the day. Other attacks in Queen's County and north Carlow came to a disastrous end, the Carlow fighting being the bloodiest. A rebel force of around a thousand men attacked Carlow town in the early hours of the day but they were enticed into a trap by the garrison. Hundreds were killed in the fighting and in the massacre that followed it, including scores who died when the houses along Tullow Street in which they took refuge were set on fire. At Hacketstown, near the Carlow border with Wicklow, the rebels were unable to take several of the strong buildings in the town and had to retreat with heavy losses. In Queen's County several hundred rebels failed to capture Monasterevin in the morning and many of them joined in another unsuccessful attack on Portarlington later in the day; once again the losses were very heavy. That afternoon, as news of the fierce fighting further up the Slaney and Barrow valleys filtered south, the commander of the garrison in Carnew, on the Wicklow border with Wexford, had his men take about thirty prisoners out of the local gaol and shoot them, one at a time. The prisoners had been arrested on suspicion of membership of the United Irishmen in the previous days and weeks.

The slaughter in Carnew brought two days of fierce fighting to a bloody end. About a thousand people had now died and both sides had already committed unspeakable atrocities, including the murder of completely innocent non-combatants. To make matters worse, in spite of the non-sectarian character of the United Irishmen, rumours of impending sectarian massacres began to circulate among both Catholics and Protestants in all parts of Leinster that had been affected by the fighting, including Dublin itself.

Saturday, 26 May 1798

On Saturday 26 May news of the rebellion was beginning to filter into counties as far from its epicentre as Wexford, Kilkenny, Tipperary and Cork as well as the Presbyterian counties of Antrim and Down. Indeed, since the Belfast and Cork mails were stopped at the beginning of the rebellion, United Irishmen in most of these counties ought to have mobilised on the twenty-fourth or, at the latest, the twenty-fifth. The fact that they did not probably arose from confusion about what the mail-coach signal meant; to some, for example, at least in Antrim and Down, it was taken to mean 'prepare' rather than 'strike'. Other local factors may have delayed the spread of the movement by the signal too. In Tipperary and Cork, for example, a combination of zealous magistrates and conciliatory Catholic gentry worked to keep the movement from taking to the field, while in Antrim and Down the Presbyterian units were by now less certain of their admiration for the French and less enthusiastic about a movement that was now so clearly dominated by Leinster. Even though it was already clear to United Irishmen in places as far apart as Cork and Antrim that a rising had begun, they had remained inactive through the twenty-fourth and twenty-fifth, leaving the Kildare, Meath and Wicklow rebels to fend for themselves.

This third day of the rebellion, nevertheless, saw important developments in Leinster. Early in the day, the advantage remained very much with the rebels, encamped in a chain of posts around the capital city. Camden and his garrison remained huddled down, hoping that any thoughts of rebellion into the city had been dampened by his deploying of soldiers in the streets, the display of dead rebels in the Castle and a public condemnation of the rebels by both the Catholic and Protestant archbishops.

One of the Viceroy's main concerns was his ignorance of the situation in Munster since the Cork road was held by the rebels. The rebels to his west, however, were on the move early in the day. Thousands of recruits flooded into the camps at Blackmoor Hill in Wicklow, Knockallen, Gibbet Rath and Timahoe in Kildare and Tara in Meath. Rebels in west Kildare overwhelmed a small garrison of yeomanry in Rathangan, one of the few villages in the county they had not yet taken, and then threatened the garrison at Edenderry, just across the border in King's County. Later in the day the commander of the Edenderry garrison got an express rider through to Camden along the Galway road to ask for reinforcements. Camden, however, remained cautious and a detachment of cavalry under Colonel Craig probed the countryside to the northwest of the city but returned without making (or diligently seeking) contact with the rebel forces.

In the meantime, about sixty miles to the south of Dublin more important developments were taking place. The United Irishmen in north Carlow and southwest Wicklow had suffered great setbacks in the battles at Carlow and Hacketstown, while around Arklow and Gorey local magistrates had tortured several men who informed on their comrades along the Wexford/Wicklow border, leaving the organisation there in complete disarray.

The situation was different in parts of Co. Wexford north of a line from New Ross to Wexford town and south of Gorey. The strong United Irishmen organisation here was led on the parish and barony level by the sons of large tenant farmers or even gentry, both Catholic and Protestant. Over the previous week, the local landowner, Lord Mountnorris, had successfully used priests to persuade many United Irishmen to surrender their weapons though the movement itself was still intact. News of the rebellion in the Kildare and Carlow areas may have reached the northernmost parts of the county as early as the twenty-fifth but it began to filter southwards rapidly on the twenty-sixth. That evening, rebel units in a broad sweep of country across central Wexford attacked the houses of magistrates and yeomen where they knew arms were being stored. Their plan was apparently to converge on two hills at Kilthomas, not far from the Carlow border, and at Oulart.

In the meantime, far to the north, the rebel camp on Tara was suddenly (and apparently with Camden's knowledge) attacked by a force of about three hundred soldiers, many of them Highlanders. The battle went on until twilight when the rebel force broke and fled, chased by the government cavalry which killed several hundred men and effectively ended the activities of the rebels in south Meath. As the rebellion spread into central Wexford then, it was being eliminated at the other end of Leinster.

Rebellion in and around Wexford (26 May-5 July)

KILDARE
WICKLOW
LAOIS
(Queen's County)
CARLOW
KILKENNY
WEXFORD
WATERFORD
ATHY
WICKLOW
Rathdrum
Hacketstown
Aughrim
ARKLOW
CARLOW
Castlecomer
Tinahely
Croghan
Shillelagh
Carnew
Limerick Hill
Kilcavan
Ballyellis
Gorey
KILKENNY
Borris
Ballyminaun Hill
Camolin
Tubberneering
Ferns
Carrigrew
Scullogue Gap
Bunclody
Kilthomas
Scarawalsh
Enniscorthy
Vinegar Hill
Oulart
Lacken Hill
New Ross
Carrigbyrne
WEXFORD
Foulkesmills
Taghmon
WATERFORD
Goff's Bridge
Duncannon
Fethard
Key government garrisons (not attacked)
Rebel camps
Key garrisons attacked but not taken
Battlesites

CHAPTER 6

The Harrow and Gibbet Rath

26 to 30 May 1798

Unaware of the slaughter at Tara, rebel units in Wexford were rapidly mobilising, raiding the houses of local gentry and yeomanry members to secure arms. On the night of Saturday 26 May, the magistrates in Wexford town, acting on information given under torture by a rebel colonel, Anthony Perry of Inch, had arrested two of the movement's colonels. This capture of Edward Fitzgerald of Newpark and Bagenal Harvey of Bargy Castle disrupted the mobilisation. By the middle of Sunday (Whit Sunday), however, close to a thousand men had joined the camp near Oulart and perhaps the same number at Kilthomas. Unlike the Kildare rebels, the Wexford units had not attempted up to this to attack large villages or towns, being satisfied to acquire as many arms as they could and wait for the militia and yeomen, stationed in the towns, to come out. In a chance encounter with a detachment of cavalry at The Harrow, three miles east of Ferns, they killed two of the yeomanry. Other than that, there was no serious confrontation and the rebels had been able to take undisputed possession of a wide stretch of country from the Carlow border near Newtownbarry, through places like Ferns, Camolin and Boolavogue, to Oulart and even as far south as Castlebridge.

Initially, things went badly for the Wexford rebels. At about ten o'clock, three hundred yeomen from Carnew launched a well-planned attack on the rebel camp on Kilthomas Hill. Although the rebels held their ground briefly, they began to give way under fire and then fled in panic, the yeoman cavalry chasing them out into the country between the camp and Ferns and killing at least a hundred of them. The rebel column was shattered and the yeomanry returned to Carnew assuming that the United Irishmen in Wexford had been destroyed.

Later in the day, however, the Wexford rebels in the eastern part of their county achieved a stunning success that suddenly gave them the momentum. At about three o'clock, five hours after the Kilthomas debacle, the rebels around

Enniscorthy in 1798: the rebels attacked along the roads from Carlow and Newtownbarry on 28 May and Lake attacked the Vinegar Hill Camp on 21 June along the road to Ferns. (Musgrave)

Oulart massed on the hill over the village. A detachment of just over a hundred militiamen from Wexford town attacked them, no doubt expecting an easy victory. Instead, in a well-planned and well-executed manoeuvre, the rebel force trapped and almost annihilated the militia, leaving only their commander and a handful of men to flee back to headquarters. The rest were cut down in the battle itself or were killed as they tried to surrender. This was the first time in the Rising that a rebel force won a pitched battle and had the chance to cut down the enemy as they fled, making this by far the most serious disaster to befall the government side anywhere in the country in the four days that the rebellion had now lasted. Later in the day, the Oulart rebels moved north to Carrigrew, another high hill in east Wexford, and began to draw hundreds of recruits to their camp; that night their leaders made plans for a more ambitious campaign in the central part of the county the following day, completely unaware that the rebel cause in Kildare and Meath had already begun to unravel.

In the midlands, too, the government forces went on the offensive. Here the

Father John Murphy, leader of the United Irishmen at the Harrow and a prominent rebel officer in Wexford throughout the Rising. This is a nineteenth-century sketch and may not be an accurate portrayal.

rebels were concentrated at the three large camps at Timahoe, Knockallen and Gibbet Rath, with smaller units at Ballitore, Blessington and Rathangan. Very early in the day troops from Carlow town attacked at Ballitore. There had been peace talks between the rebels there and the Athy commander during the night; these had ended in confusion and the commander was unaware of the Carlow garrison's move against the rebel position. The Carlow troops swept into the town first and scattered the rebels (who were surprised by their arrival); a short time after they had departed the soldiers from Athy came in and killed anyone they found. A few hours later, Dundas, finally emboldened to leave the safety of Naas, swept down on Blessington and overwhelmed a rebel camp there. Later in the day, after they had first beaten off an attack by a cavalry unit from Tullamore, the rebel garrison in Rathangan was suddenly attacked from the direction of Dublin by a militia unit that had dared push into the heart of Co. Kildare, causing the rebels to lose possession of that town too. Then, in what must have been a very welcome development to Dundas's ears, a deputation from the large rebel camp at Knockallen announced that they were willing to begin negotiations for dispersal. Dundas must certainly have assumed that the rebellion was on the point of expiring.

Monday, 28 May 1798

On Monday 28 May, the fifth day of rebellion, the United Irishmen's cause in Wexford and the midlands continued to develop in opposite directions and there was still no sign of an uprising in either Munster or Ulster. In Kildare, Dundas now clearly had the upper hand. He made no moves against the three rebel strongholds but consolidated his gains in the eastern fringes of the county and continued to negotiate with the Knockallen camp. However, extremist government supporters in Dublin, confident of victory now that they knew of developments in Meath and Kildare and unaware as yet of what had happened in Wexford, began to demand a more severe approach than Dundas had adopted. Even Camden grew impatient and sent one of his most highly-respected officers, Colonel Lambert Walpole, to Naas to warn Dundas against accepting anything but unconditional surrender from the Knockallen rebels. That evening, increasingly concerned at what Dundas was doing and obviously now far less concerned about the safety of the capital, Camden even sent Lake, the commander-in-chief himself, out to Kildare to toughen Dundas's stand. The midlands commander was unaware of developments in Wexford. Neither did he know that General Sir James Duff, the government's commander in Limerick, had that very morning begun a hundred mile march across the centre of the country, with four hundred men and six cannon, using commandeered carts to gain time. Duff was frustrated at the indecision of the Southern Division commander, General Sir James Stewart, and had concluded that no rising would take place in Munster. Therefore he decided that he should now attack the midlands rebels in the rear.

By now, the situation was very different in Wexford where government forces were in rapid retreat. As Duff was marching from Limerick and as Dundas was still trying to persuade the Knockallen rebels to disperse, the Carrigrew rebels, now swelled to perhaps two or three thousand men, swept down from their hilltop camp, marching first west to Camolin, then south to Ferns and from there on to Scarawalsh Bridge, two miles north of Enniscorthy. Everywhere the small garrisons fled before them, leaving behind large quantities of arms, including carbines sent to Co. Wexford for the yeomanry and huge numbers of pikes that the magistrates had previously collected. Shortly after midday, the rebels launched a frontal assault on Enniscorthy. The largest town any rebel force had attacked up to this point, and with dismal results, was Naas and even smaller towns and villages in Kildare had proven to be difficult to take. However, the rebel army that threw itself at Enniscorthy numbered in the thousands and after several hours of fierce fighting the garrison abandoned the town, fleeing south towards Wexford town. Several hundred men, most of them rebels, were killed in the struggle for Enniscorthy but that evening hundreds more United Irishmen and men who were now persuaded to consider themselves United Irishmen came into

Cruickshank's representation of the Vinegar Hill camp: This says more about the ultra-loyalist sense of what the rebellion was about than what the camp was really like.

the camp. As this was happening, groups of rebels scoured the town for those they considered their enemies and killed many on the spot. The fearsome brutality that both sides had exhibited in the midlands was being repeated now in the southeast.

Tuesday, 29 May 1798

Throughout 29 May the Wexford rebels maintained their momentum. Their colonels and captains at Vinegar Hill watched with satisfaction as units came in from all over the central part of the county as well as from the borderlands of Wicklow and Wexford to the north. The rebel army swelled to at least ten thousand men during the day and by evening almost all the colonels were present, with the exception of those from the very south of the county. However, the adjutant-general for the county, Bagenal Harvey, and two important colonels, Edward Fitzgerald and John Henry Colclough, were still prisoners in Wexford town. In a desperate gamble, the garrison sent Fitzgerald and Colclough north to the Vinegar Hill camp to ask the rebels to disperse peacefully. The insurgents rejected the overture contemptuously and responded to what they saw as a sign of weakness on the part of the garrison by marching southwards, encamping on Forth Mountain, southwest of the town, by nightfall. The United Irishmen of Wexford had now taken possession of the entire central half of their county and had trapped its largest garrison between their camp and the sea. Unaware of what had been taking place behind their backs in the midlands, they were now on the verge of complete victory within their own county.

That same day in Kildare, however, events produced a triumph for the government side and for Dundas and his policy. That afternoon he had gone out to the Knockallen camp, accompanied by only a small bodyguard, and had personally negotiated the peaceful dispersal of the entire rebel force. Lake, who arrived too late to stop him, was incensed and Duff, who was now in Tipperary and still on his way to Kildare, was completely in the dark about what was happening. At this juncture, with Tara taken by force and Knockallen by persuasion, only three rebel camps of any size were still in place near Dublin: the Blackmoor camp in the Wicklow mountains, the Timahoe camp in north Kildare, probably the smallest of the three, and the Gibbet Rath camp near Newbridge. Dundas had already decided to open negotiations with the Gibbet Rath group next day; should they disperse the midlands rebellion would be effectively at an end.

To everyone's surprise Ulster had remained quiet up to now, in spite of the fact that the Belfast mail coach was the first to be stopped on the twenty-third. On 29 May however, the Ulster Directory held a meeting in Armagh which turned into a fierce war of words between the leadership, who had thus far been very slow to call for a rebellion, and more hot-headed men anxious to start an immediate uprising. The militants won the struggle, voted the Directory out and a new one in. They then passed a resolution that the adjutants-general of Antrim and Down should meet the next day to finalise plans for mobilisation in their two counties. Camden was unaware of this meeting but had just received news from his spies in Ulster that something was afoot there too. This news was a cause for concern because, even though the Leinster rebellion seemed to be expiring, the Ulster Presbyterians were well-known to have begun the United Irishmen movement and, in spite of Lake's disarming of them in 1797, the government still feared them greatly.

Wednesday, 30 May 1798

The following day marked the beginning of the second week of rebellion. For the Co. Wexford rebels it was a third day of spectacular success while the rebellion continued to unravel in the midlands and the United Irishmen of eastern Ulster continued to hesitate. In Wexford, the central event was the capture of Wexford town, the county seat and the largest garrison – some twelve

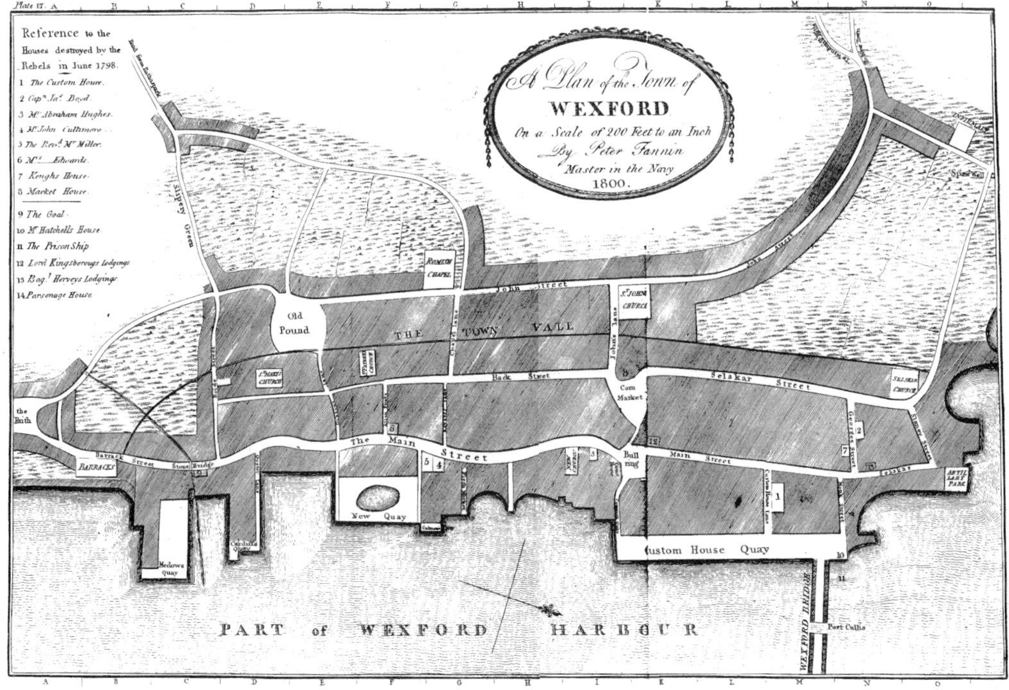

Street map of Wexford town as it was in the 1790s, with buildings of significance in 1798 marked: John Street was an artisan suburb and this was the main route in and out of the town; the garrison escaped along Barrack Street on 20 May. (Musgrave)

hundred men – in the county. The garrison had waited all night for help to come from Duncannon Fort but when a relieving column of militia was ambushed a few miles from the town just before dawn and a brief sally to attack the rebel camp proved futile, the garrison commander, Colonel Maxwell, decided to evacuate. He deceived the rebel commanders with a bogus initiative for negotiations and slipped past the rebel camp with almost his entire force and their arms and ammunition at around midday, reaching the safety of Duncannon Fort that night. By the afternoon the rebels realised what had happened and took possession of the town. That evening the rebels were in undisputed possession of all of the county, apart from a chain of towns around its northern and western perimeter: Gorey, Newtownbarry, New Ross and Duncannon. The Wexford colonels and their adjutant-general, Bagenal Harvey, who was now free, were certainly aware of the rebel setbacks in north Carlow and south Wicklow but they are likely to have been optimistic about developments further north in Kildare and Dublin and very likely expected that their feats had been matched in many other parts of the country. Ironically though, as the Wexford rebels were taking possession of their county capital, the Kildare rebels, the last group outside Wexford still to have a formidable force, were being annihilated.

Dundas was once again at the centre of the affair. That morning he had carried on indirect talks with the Gibbet Rath camp. Unknown to him, however, Duff and his four hundred men and six cannon had earlier entered Kildare town and, finding it ruined and abandoned, pushed on towards the camp at Gibbet Rath. Around the middle of the day Dundas had finally persuaded the rebels to lay down their arms and they had begun to do so. At this point, Duff came in sight of the rath from the west and, either because he was unaware of what was happening or had a shot fired at him from the rebel ranks or simply allowed his own or his soldiers' blood-lust free rein, his column attacked the nearly helpless United Irishmen on the hill. In the resulting massacre hundreds of rebels, many of them already unarmed, were cut down without mercy and those who managed to escape fled in all directions. A few managed to make their way across the county boundary into Wicklow and hid in the hills with the various Wicklow units. Most made their way home and by nightfall, as the Wexford rebels celebrated their victory in the narrow main street of their town, the entire rebellion outside of Wexford had dissolved, only the small camps at Timahoe Bog in north Kildare and on Blackmoor Hill in north Wicklow still remaining. Arguably, had it not been for the Battle of Oulart two days before, the entire uprising might now have ended, particularly since the adjutants-general of Antrim and Down, in spite of the resolutions of the previous day, had decided to wait for more definite news from Leinster before moving. From the vantage point of Dublin Castle that night, the rebellion had come and gone and the government had easily prevailed.

CHAPTER 7

THE BOYS OF WEXFORD

31 May to 4 June 1798

Over the five days between the morning of Thursday 31 May and the evening of Monday 4 June, the rebellion became exclusively a Wexford affair. United Irish units were nowhere else in the field apart from the small scattered detachments in the hills of Wicklow and in the bogs of north Kildare. During this period the Wexfordmen went from initial exuberance at the prospect of being part of a triumphant revolutionary movement, through a period of crisis once the reality of their situation began to become apparent and finally to renewed hope after they achieved a stunning defeat over the government's first serious attempt to crush them. By the night of 4 June, in fact, they were at the pinnacle of their success in military terms; they were also, however, still completely alone in rebellion.

Thursday, 31 May 1798

The morning after their capture of the town, the Wexford rebels awoke to what they must have thought was the new world they had created. There was tremendous confusion in the narrow streets although far less violence against loyalists than had occurred two days earlier in Enniscorthy. Ominously though, several bands did go around the town arresting those they suspected of loyalist sympathies and others scoured the countryside roundabout. Later in the day, the United Irish officers restored order and called their immense army, now numbering perhaps fifteen thousand men (and women) out to Windmill Hill, a high point just to the west of the town, where they held a council of war. After a lengthy, even heated, debate they set up a command structure with Bagenal Harvey as commander-in-chief for the county and with the various United Irish colonels in charge of barony battalions. They also decided to split their force into two divisions. One was to march north led by 'colonels' such as Edward Roche, Edward Fitzgerald, Anthony Perry and four Catholic priests, all of whom had fallen out of favour with their bishop – fathers John Murphy, Mogue Kearns, Philip Roche and Michael Murphy. The other column was to move

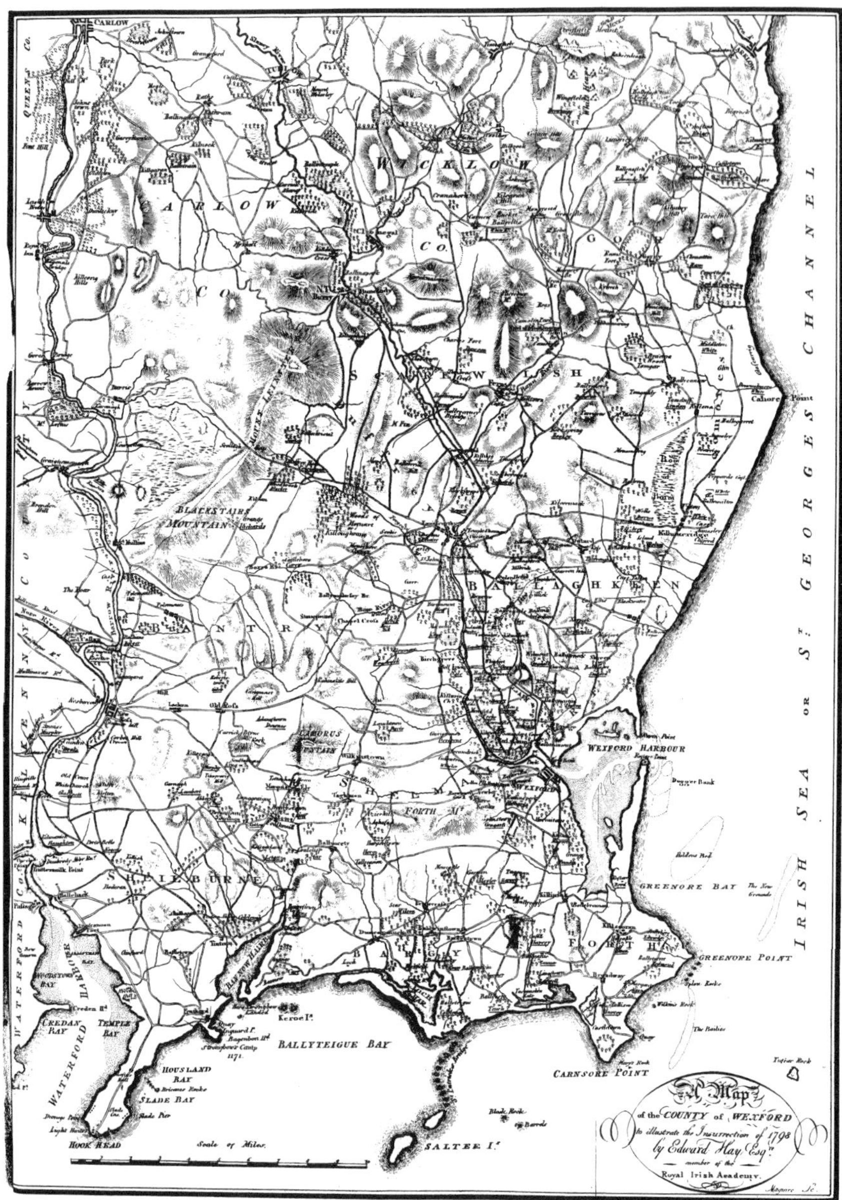

Edward Hay's map of County Wexford, showing main hills, gentry residences and roadways as they were around 1798.

towards the west, led by Harvey himself, supported by Thomas Cloney, John Kelly and John Henry Colclough. The intention at this point appears to have been to reduce the government garrisons around the perimeter of the county and to revive the rebellion further afield by example or even to await contact from the rebel forces they presumed were still in a strong position in the midlands and in Wicklow. The northern division marched back to Vinegar Hill that afternoon, part of it camping there and the other part continuing on to Carrigrew. The division under Bagenal Harvey made less progress, partly because he spent several hours attempting to reassure old loyalists who had not been arrested that they would have a place in the new regime, but most of this division had reached the village of Taghmon by nightfall and camped there.

There was unquestionably an air of confidence, even complacency, about the Wexford rebels at this point. Harvey had been very casual in his preparations for the march west and several of his colonels and their men had not even bothered to join him at Taghmon. Their situation was perilous though. By this stage, Camden and Lake had received word of the extent of the Wexford rebellion and, though they did not realise Wexford town had been taken, it looked to them less like a mere extension of the badly organised insurrection in north Carlow and south Wicklow and more like an uprising on the scale of Kildare.

Elsewhere in the country, the situation seemed to be under control. The roads to Munster and Connaught were open again with no sign of an uprising in those areas and, in spite of the report of a 'buzz' in Ulster the day before, there had been no significant developments there either. The Ulster movement continued to be divided between its officer class, hesitant to make a move, and its rank-and-file anxious to seize the moment and rise. This tug-of-war would go on for several days more.

Friday, 1 June 1798

On 1 June, the Wexford rebels experienced their very first setbacks as the government forces made tentative moves to crush them. The southern division, which had camped at Taghmon the night before, was slow to leave in the morning and only managed to reach Carrickbyrne Hill, a high point about six miles from New Ross, by evening. The northern division was more decisive. Its Vinegar Hill column, under Fr Mogue Kearns, attacked Newtownbarry early in the day but was defeated with the loss of perhaps a hundred men after government reinforcements arrived at a critical point in the battle. A few hours later, an advance party from Carrigrew marched north towards Gorey and unexpectedly met a detachment of militia moving south from the town. Again the rebels were caught unawares and lost well over a hundred men in a pitched battle in the fields around Ballyminaun Hill, just north of Ballycanew. By evening the remnants of the columns that had marched on Newtownbarry and Gorey were back at their camps on Vinegar Hill and Carrigrew where the rebel officers in both places were forced to reassess their situation now that resistance from the government garrisons on the perimeter of the county had turned out to be so spirited.

For their part, Camden and Lake, still unaware of the fall of Wexford town, decided to move. Lake resolved to launch a three-pronged attack on north Co. Wexford, one column under General Loftus to march through Gorey, a detachment under Colonel Walpole to come from central Kildare through Carnew, and a third column, under Lord Ancram, to move south to Newtownbarry and to approach the rebel strongholds from the west. Lake also sent instructions to General Johnson at Waterford asking him to move to New Ross to strengthen the garrison there. By evening, the manoeuvre was still in its early stages but Lake was obviously now ready to focus his attention on the only rebellion left and was probably confident that he could crush it in a matter of days.

The course of events in Ulster ensured that Wexford's United Irishmen would continue to be alone in their resistance. The colonels of the Antrim organisation met at Parkgate to discuss their situation. Once again though, despite vigorous calls for an immediate rising from among some of the leaders themselves and from rank-and-file members who had contact with them, they chose caution and dispersed that evening without making a firm decision. Clearly, news from Leinster was still not encouraging enough for them to take the chance of initiating a rebellion likely to fail.

Saturday, 2 June 1798

On 2 June, a full week since the Wexford rebels had mobilised, the rebel camps at Carrigrew, Vinegar Hill and Carrickbyrne remained inactive. The rebel leaders were possibly chastened by the defeats of the day before and preferred to consolidate their position, preparing their men for future battles rather than risk pushing them forward against an enemy whose strength was unknown. By adopting this cautious strategy, they allowed the initiative to slip into the hands of the government and during the day Walpole, Loftus and Ancram all moved steadily closer to the borders of the county while orders to march on New Ross reached Johnson in Waterford.

In Wexford town itself and in the large portion of Co. Wexford now under rebel control a rudimentary system of emergency government had been set up. A governing Directory, headed by Matthew Keogh, a former British officer, a Protestant and a colonel of the United Irishmen, was set up in the town. Keogh was joined in this capacity by, among others, Dr Ebenezer Jacob, the former mayor, also a Protestant, and by Edward Hay, the son of a prominent Catholic landlord, who took charge of manufacturing munitions. Arrangements were made to supply the town and the camps with food and small companies of rebel volunteers served as a police force. Outside the town there was great confusion but the rebels organised small parties to guard all the important crossroads and a communication system was established to link what was now functioning as the capital of a sort of 'Wexford Republic', with its troops in the camps several miles away.

In spite of the apparent good order in Wexford town and elsewhere, the rebels at Vinegar Hill seem to have persisted in their policy of rounding up and executing loyalists. As on previous days, several were put to death on the summit of the hill after quick trials and the rebel search parties continued to scour the countryside. The camps at Carrigrew and Carrickbyrne did not witness such scenes but they also sent out search parties looking for loyalists. Those arrested by the Carrickbyrne rebels up to this point (and the number was probably one or two dozen by the end of the day) were confined at a farm in the nearby townland of Scullabogue.

There was still no rising in Ulster but nonetheless this would turn out to be an important day for the Presbyterian United Irishmen. The Antrim colonels met once more but again could not agree to rise and by the afternoon the faction that favoured waiting until the French landed got the upper hand. As several of these men were on the way home, they were confronted at a place called Ballyeaston by a crowd of rank-and-file members who hurled abuse and rocks at them and condemned them for their cowardice. At this point a young Belfast officer, Henry Joy McCracken, seized the initiative and began to garner support for a rising with or without French help. It would take him and his supporters several days to bring their plans to fruition but the tide in favour of rebellion had now finally turned in the region.

Sunday, 3 June 1798

Next day, news of plans for a rising reached United Irishmen across Antrim and Down and even into Armagh and Tyrone – the pikes were taken out of the thatch once more. It did not take long for Camden's spies in Ulster to warn him of an imminent insurrection. However, the government's focus was still on Wexford. During the Sunday, Walpole and Loftus made steady progress and by the afternoon Walpole reached Carnew, Loftus got as far as Arklow while Ancram had already arrived in Newtownbarry. Later in the day Loftus pushed on to Gorey and was joined there by Walpole that evening, a bitter dispute breaking out between them over Walpole's precise role in the coming battle. Evidently, Walpole wanted the largest share of the fighting – and of the glory – for himself.

That day the rebel leaders made no moves. At Carrigrew the men spent the day drilling and encouraging even more recruits to join them. That night, however, a spy rode out from Gorey to tell them that an attack on their camp was

Wexford town in 1796, viewed from the north bank of the estuary: The toll house on this end of the bridge was burned when the rebels took the town (30 May); the massacre of loyalists (20 June) and executions of former rebels (21 June on) took place at the town end of the bridge. Windmill Hill, the rallying point for the rebels, overlooks the town on the horizon.

imminent. They decided to take the fight to the enemy, breaking camp early next day and meeting the government soldiers in the open before they could be surrounded.

In Wexford town, the situation in the country as a whole was becoming clearer. The failure to break through the government strongholds around the county was ominous. In addition, news of the failure of the rebellion in Dublin and perhaps of at least some of the defeats in the midlands had reached them from a prisoner: Lord Kingsborough, the commander of the North Cork militia, who had left Dublin by ship a few days previously to join his men whom he believed to be still in Wexford. His ship had been captured off Wexford and the prisoner, an important prize, would have given rebel leaders like Keogh and Hay the news from outside and left them in no doubt about their isolation.

Monday, 4 June 1798

In most parts of Ireland, there was little change in the situation on 4 June. The post-rebellion repression that had gone on in Kildare, Meath and Wicklow for five days continued unabated and there was still no sign of a rebel movement in Munster or Connaught. In Ulster, government commanders, including General Nugent who was in charge of the entire northern district, saw no signs of impending rebellion. For their part, the Ulster United Irishmen, now being increasingly directed by men like McCracken, were indeed readying themselves for mobilisation but spent the day, under conditions of martial law, trying to get word of their plans to units that had not yet heard of them. There were, however, dramatic developments in Co. Wexford. In the southern half of the county, Bagenal Harvey had an army of at least ten thousand men gathered at Carrickbyrne by the afternoon and he finally got ready to lead them on New Ross. That very morning, however, General Johnson and his Waterford column crossed the bridge into the town, bringing the garrison's strength up to about two thousand, and Harvey's opportunity to attack the town while it was still lightly garrisoned slipped through his hands. However, the long-expected assault on the town was now imminent and it must have been clear to all concerned that this would be a vital test for both sides. In the northern part of the county, the rival armies were also on the march. A few hours after dawn, Loftus and Walpole led their army of around twelve hundred men southwards out of Gorey with the intention of attacking the rebel camp on Carrigrew, which was now at least ten thousand strong.

At the same time, Lord Ancram moved several miles into the county from Newtownbarry and took up position at Ferns to cut off the rebel retreat. The rebels also broke camp that morning and marched towards Gorey, directly at the approaching soldiers. A short distance outside Gorey, Loftus and Walpole split their forces, each taking a separate road. At Tubberneering, about two miles from Carrigrew, the rebel vanguard suddenly encountered Walpole and his force. On the rebel side, Edward Roche hurriedly took charge of the situation and mounted a fierce attack, lasting about half an hour, in which Walpole himself and around fifty of his men were killed. Loftus was confused about what was happening and did not get to Tubberneering until Walpole's column was in full retreat and the rebels were marching on to Gorey, taking the now unguarded town and setting up camp on a hill just to the south. Loftus eventually approached the hill from the direction of Tubberneering but soon retreated back southwards and led his men first south, then west, across the hilly country of northwest Wexford to Carnew and then on to Tullow in Co. Carlow. When he realised what had happened, Lord Ancram pulled back to Newtownbarry. Meantime, the garrison at Arklow, convinced that the rebel army would overwhelm them next day, abandoned the town and during the evening retreated all the way to Wicklow town.

That night, as they settled into their new camp on Gorey Hill, the rebel leaders watched with delight as scores of United Irishmen who had been hiding out in the hills of south Wicklow now came in and joined them. The moment must have been uplifting for men like Roche, Perry, Fitzgerald and Michael and John Murphy. They had now recovered from the setbacks of four days earlier and had swept their enemies from all of north Wexford. They knew that the government's efforts to destroy them had collapsed but they did not seem to realise that the entire southern third of Co. Wicklow had been thrown open to them.

Meanwhile, in southern Wexford, Bagenal Harvey completed his plans for the attack on New Ross and during the evening his huge army marched, a battalion at a time, west to Corbet Hill, a ridge looking down on the town. By nightfall, thousands of rebels were in position to attack while the town's garrison below them dug trenches and made earthworks to defend it. Johnson and Harvey were both probably unaware of what had happened at Tubberneering and Gorey earlier in the day. Had they known, they would have better understood the importance of the battle that was about to take place. Should the rebel army take New Ross next morning, Co. Wexford might well become the springboard for the spread of the rebellion to much of the southeastern part of the country. To Harvey at New Ross and the other rebel leaders at Gorey, their campaign was only part of a larger struggle, the focal point of which was still, as far as they knew, places like Kildare, Queen's County and Tipperary. They were unaware that their comrades had been cowering in defeat in such places now for five days and they were unaware also of what, if anything, was happening in Ulster.

CHAPTER 8

THE DARKEST DAYS

5 to 6 June 1798

At daybreak on Tuesday 5 June, Bagenal Harvey sent a lone rider down the slopes of Corbet Hill towards the government soldiers dug in on the edge of New Ross. The horseman, Michael Furlong, a prominent young rebel, carried a white flag and a letter, written by Harvey and addressed to Johnson, calling for the peaceful surrender of the town. When Furlong got within range of the troops, they opened fire and killed him, in spite of his white flag. The rebels massed on the hillside above were incensed and Harvey and his officers, abandoning all hope of a bloodless victory, immediately began to plan for a full frontal assault.

At about five o'clock, with the sun coming up, the rebel army began to file into position. The garrison numbered about two thousand well-armed men and their trenches and other defences ran around the eastern and southern perimeter of the town. The medieval wall was still standing in most places and Harvey decided to throw his men at the three gates at the eastern, southeastern and southern sides. At the word to advance, three columns of insurgents began to move forward but the attack did not go well at first. In the central part of the front, a battalion led by John Kelly of Killanne, advanced to well within musket range of the central or Three Bullet gate, their assigned objective. But a battalion led by Thomas Cloney that was coming behind them faltered and halted their advance while at the same time the entire column on the rebel right, led by John Henry Colclough, stopped completely, the nerve of many of the men evidently lost. Johnson sent out a detachment of dragoons to take advantage of this situation but the rebel battalions under Kelly and Cloney drove them back with the loss of some twenty men, their commander included. However, the column led by John Henry Colclough had begun to retreat up the hill, eventually abandoning the battlefield altogether and taking no further part in the fighting.

The other two rebel columns pressed on with the attack. At about six o'clock, after a fierce exchange of musket fire and several pike charges, the defenders began to fall back and soon abandoned their trenches and earthworks on the southern and along most of the eastern side of the town. The rebel forces

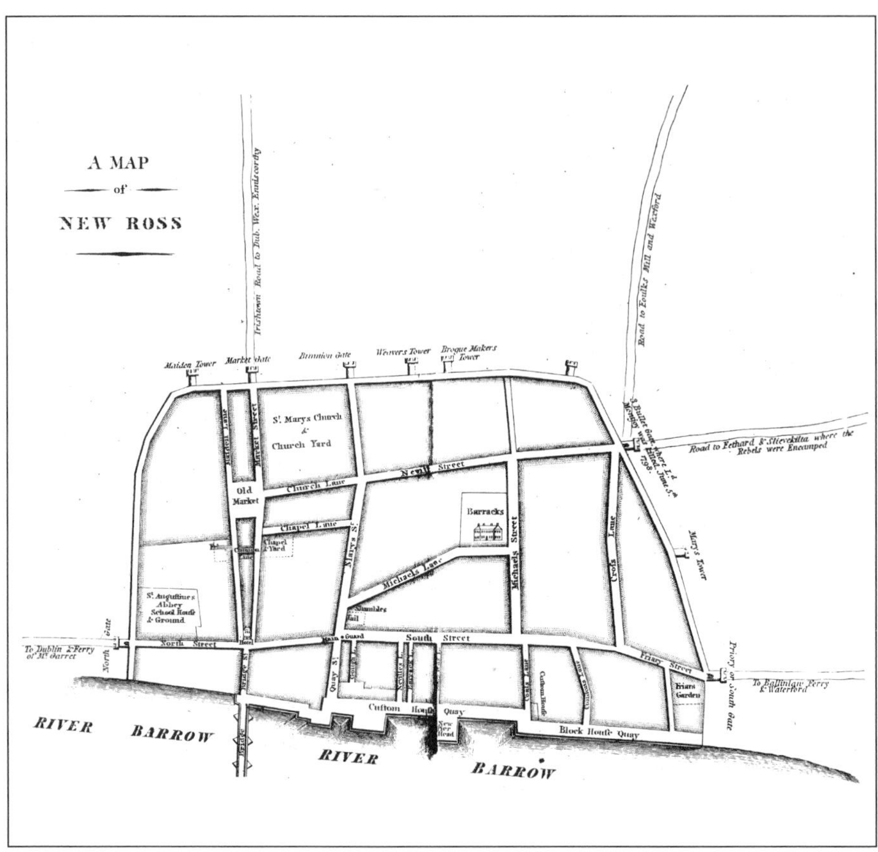

Street map of New Ross in 1798: The rebel attack came at Three Bullet and Priory gates and at their point of furthest advance the rebels had taken the entire southern part of the town to just beyond the line formed by Quay Street and Mary's Street. (Musgrave)

took full advantage and within about half-an-hour Kelly's men had reached well into the town and had the barracks surrounded. The group attacking from the south, led by John Boxwell, another Protestant rebel officer, had made their way into the southern end of South Street. Kelly was wounded at this point, his thigh shattered by a bullet, and he had to be carried back out of the town. This was a big loss but the rebels pressed on under Boxwell and Cloney, making steady progress along the north-south streets. At this point, Harvey moved down to the Three Bullet gate to direct the attack.

By about eight o'clock, three hours into the battle, the tide seemed to be running in favour of the rebels. They had lost hundreds of men but casualties on the garrison side were heavy too. The most advanced rebel units were fighting to take possession of the Pig Market which would allow them to cut off a large part of the garrison stationed at the Market Gate, which Colclough's battalion had failed to attack, from the main body of defenders concentrated near the bridge. Indeed, at about this point, large sections of the garrison had already retreated to the Kilkenny side of the river. An attack on them here by Kilkenny United Irish units might have completely ended the battle but, although these units had mobilised around Glenmore and Inishtioge that morning, they did not march on New Ross and thus gave the garrison a critical break.

Some time between eight and nine o'clock the rebels inside the town lost the initiative, either because they were exhausted and confused by the smoke which filled much of the town or because they believed that the day was theirs. The respite was enough for Johnson to convince his men that they should counter-attack. He led them back across the bridge and launched a fierce sortie that caught Boxwell's and Cloney's men completely by surprise. The fighting went on for about an hour, by which time the garrison soldiers had pushed their way back to the Three Bullet and Priory gates. For several hours more the rebels tried to regain the initiative in small pike charges and in a running musketry battle but their efforts failed. By about one o'clock in the afternoon, they pulled back to Corbet Hill and then marched out along the road to Carrickbyrne, exhausted and utterly demoralised. Behind them they left perhaps as many as two thousand men dead, in addition to thousands of weapons and five of the six artillery pieces they had taken to the battle. John Boxwell was among the dead and John Kelly, while he survived his wound, was so badly hurt that he could take no further part in the rebellion. The garrison, in contrast had lost about two hundred men and had held the town.

Historians have frequently, and rightly, regarded the Battle of New Ross as the critical battle in the war in Wexford. Had the rebels been victorious they might have been able to rally United Irishmen in western counties to their cause. The fact that some Kilkenny units did respond to the attack on the town, albeit half-heartedly, supports this. A victory at New Ross, coming on the heels of that at Tubberneering the day before and the prospect of imminent revolution in Ulster, would certainly have prolonged the war, even if it might not have altered the eventual outcome.

The Battle of New Ross is important also because it produced more numerous and more brutal atrocities than had been seen in what had already been a brutal war up to that point. During their counter-offensive, the garrison soldiers took to bayoneting and shooting captured and wounded rebels and set fire to a four-storey building in Mary Street in which about seventy rebels were taking shelter, perhaps because they were wounded, burning them all to death. Such merciless atrocities were not, of course, the monopoly of government soldiers in this war. The rebels at Oulart had shown the same propensity to kill prisoners, but

A scene from the Battle of New Ross, as recreated by George Cruickshank, the London illustrator, in the 1840s. The caption of the original reads: 'Come on, boys, her mouth's stopt!' This incident may never have happened.

at New Ross the soldiers also apparently shot and bayoneted non-combatants who had to come out into the streets because their houses had caught fire in the fighting. The numbers killed in this fashion are uncertain but estimates run into the hundreds.

News of the atrocities was carried eastwards from an early hour. Accompanying it was a message, sent by whom it is not clear but almost certainly not the rebel leaders, that the prisoners at Scullabogue should be put to death. The captain of the guard at first refused to act on these instructions but eventually seems to have been convinced to carry them out. At around nine or ten o'clock, he had his men shoot about thirty of the prisoners on the lawn in front of the farmhouse. Then the rebel guards set fire to a barn in which the rest of the prisoners, at least eighty in number, including several old men, women and children, were being held. Everyone in the building died. Rebel parties had committed many murders during the conflict up to this point but they had never killed on this scale and they had never killed women and children. When they reached their camp later in the afternoon, Bagenal Harvey and the rest of his officers must surely have realised that the idealism of the Wexford United

Irishmen had died that day, along with any chance of victory.

Far to the north in Ulster, none of this was known of nor would it be for a long time yet and McCracken and his officers spent the day of the Battle of New Ross spreading word of the impending rising. Things were developing well for the militants now although on this particular afternoon the movement suffered a severe blow when Rev William Steele Dickson, the United Irishmen's adjutant-general in Co. Down, was arrested. Apart from this though, no government crackdown had yet taken place even though the movement was still peppered with spies and General Nugent was aware that plans for a rising were being finalised.

For its part, the government was still focusing its attention on Wexford. News of the disaster at Tubberneering and the subsequent retreats of government forces had reached Lake by way of an express rider before dawn. He was stunned by the details but reacted quickly. That afternoon he had Lieutenant-General Needham leave Loughlinstown camp, just south of Dublin, at the head of about a thousand men, by far the largest force to be despatched to Wexford thus far. Needham commandeered carts before leaving and used them to speed his journey. Amazingly, he had reached Wicklow town by nightfall and camped there until dawn. This put him within a day's march of Arklow and in a good position to move into the town in advance of the rebels who were still on Gorey Hill, awaiting a fresh supply of gunpowder which they had requested that day from Wexford town. They were also patrolling the countryside around the town for signs of government troops, unaware both of the proximity of Needham or of that day's disaster at New Ross. Most importantly, they had no idea what was happening in the little Presbyterian communities of Antrim and Down, one hundred and fifty miles to the north.

Wednesday, 6 June 1798

On the following day, McCracken and his Ulster United Irishmen finally decided to strike the next morning. They had a well-conceived plan. Rebel units would mobilise in their respective districts, rendezvous at several larger centres and then converge on Antrim town, where the county's magistrates were due to meet that day. This would allow them to capture some of the most important government figures in the county and at the same time take a strategically important town from which they could launch a larger attack on Belfast. They assumed that similar mobilisations would take place in other eastern and central Ulster counties and that all the United Irish armies would eventually coalesce to march on Dublin and link up with the United Irishmen forces in Leinster. They were only vaguely aware of the setbacks in Dublin and in the midlands but McCracken and his lieutenants seem to have been sufficiently confident of

Cruickshank's illustration of the massacre at Scullabogue: A smaller group of rebels than this illustration suggests may have been involved.

successes elsewhere in the country and of the prospect of a French landing to take what surely looked like a considerable risk at this point. As had happened in the Leinster mobilisation two weeks earlier, though, the spy network did its work for the government in Ulster and by that evening government officers in south Antrim, including the governor of the Antrim town garrison, were aware that an attack was planned for the next day.

In the meantime, the Wexford rebels spent the day in their camps, stunned perhaps by the events of the day before. At Carrickbyrne, Harvey tried desperately to redeem the situation. His army had largely melted away and he tried to rebuild it by issuing a directive, printed on a small printing press in Wexford town, ordering all able-bodied men to report to the various rebel camps. It was his effort at a mass conscription in the style of revolutionary France and it suggested a leader who realised all was lost unless he could rally his followers to one final desperate effort. Harvey still did not know of how badly things had gone elsewhere in the country but all the evidence had been pointing for days to a disaster for the movement to his north and west.

Belatedly, Harvey also tried to ensure that rebel troops would avoid atrocities by decreeing the death penalty for those who murdered prisoners. For a week now the Protestant community in southern Wexford had been beset by rumours of an impending sectarian massacre. The fact that the United Irishmen were non-sectarian and that Harvey himself, as well as several other leading rebel officers, including even some of those involved in the Scullabogue killings, were Protestants seems to have done little to quell these rumours.

In the northern part of the county, things were no better. At the main camp on Gorey Hill, Roche, Perry, Fitzgerald and John and Michael Murphy, unaware of the disaster at New Ross, were still waiting for the gunpowder they had requested. They sent out patrols towards the west but these learned little of the whereabouts of their nearest enemy. Needham, however, was on the move. He left Wicklow town in the morning with his column of a thousand men, arriving in Arklow in the afternoon despite having to stop several times to prevent the yeomanry from devastating the country on either side of the road as they marched. Once in the town he immediately set his men to digging a network of trenches around its southern perimeter and by evening Arklow presented a formidable barrier to any rebel attempt to march up the east coast towards Dublin. Not realising that this formed part of the original United Irishmen's plan for the rising and lacking the ammunition to mount any such attack, the Wexford men let slip a golden opportunity to threaten the capital from the south without ever quite realising that they had had it.

By the evening of Wednesday 6 June, then, at the end of two full weeks of rebellion, only Co. Wexford was not in government hands and this had been the case for a week. However, the conflagration which the establishment had feared above all, an uprising among the Presbyterians of Ulster, was within hours of breaking out. And if there was one thing that might yet save the rebellion at this late stage, it was a successful uprising in Ulster, especially when a powerful rebel movement was still active in south Leinster.

Rebel Campaign in Ulster (7-13 June)
DERRY
(LONDONDERRY)
Garvagh
Kilrea
DERRY
(LONDONDERRY)
Maghera
ANTRIM
Ballymena
Larne
Randalstown
ANTRIM
Bangor
Hollywood
BELFAST
Newtownards
Lisburn
Comber
Saintfield
Ballynahinch
Portaferry
DONEGAL
TYRONE
FERMANAGH
ARMAGH
DOWN
MONAGHAN
Key towns not attacked
Towns attacked but not taken
Towns taken by rebels

CHAPTER 9

PRESBYTERIAN REBELLION AND THE ATTACK ON ARKLOW

7 to 9 June 1798

On Thursday 7 June, the United Irishmen of Ulster finally rose. The first action took place at Larne on the Antrim coast, about twenty miles from Belfast. Local rebels mobilised during the hours after midnight and mounted a surprise attack on the small garrison at about two in the morning. The soldiers were soon driven back into the barracks in the centre of the town where they held out for several hours and eventually managed to retreat safely to Carrickfergus, ten miles from Belfast. The Larne rebels then marched out in the direction of Antrim town and were joined by other units which had neutralised or bypassed the garrisons of small towns nearby.

By early that morning larger rebel columns were formed at rendezvous points all over the central and southern parts of the county. They attacked and overwhelmed government forces at Randalstown and Ballymena and by afternoon were converging in large numbers on Donegore Hill, overlooking Antrim town, McCracken's main objective for the day. By mid-afternoon he had about four thousand men on the hill overlooking the town and perhaps the same number from more distant parts of the county were on the way to join him there. This was by far the most impressive rebel mobilisation to take place in the rebellion up to then; the Wexford rebels at Kilthomas and Oulart did not exceed one thousand on 27 May. In addition, the northern rebels had been extraordinarily efficient in their conduct and relatively restrained in their treatment of prisoners.

However, the attempt to seize Antrim town turned into a disaster. Rebel units were still on the way towards the town when McCracken decided to attack with the force he already had. The garrison of about three hundred men put up stiff resistance but they were finally forced back, being eventually rescued from rout by a reinforcement of dragoons. At one point, the dragoons themselves began to retreat but the Randalstown rebels, arriving in the town at this stage and seeing the dragoons rushing towards them, thought they were charging rather than retreating and began to flee in disorder. The setback had a domino effect. Seeing the Randalstown column broken, McCracken's men lost some of their resolve and when more government reinforcements, sent by Nugent, arrived they too faltered and were driven back out of the town, retreating to Donegore Hill. Word of the reverse spread rapidly and by nightfall many of the units coming into Antrim town from outlying areas turned about and dispersed to their homes, thinking the cause was lost.

That evening, the garrison in Antrim began a campaign of terror like those which had already taken place many times in the south, summarily executing anyone they suspected of being a rebel and dumping their bodies into mass graves. There is even a story of a wounded rebel being deliberately buried alive with the dead. Rebel losses in the fighting for Antrim itself were relatively light, one estimate putting them as only twenty killed, but perhaps as many as three hundred were executed by the end of the day. Later the same day, the rebellion spread to the eastern part of Co. Derry and a force of perhaps five thousand rebels attacked but failed to take Maghera. Rebel mobilisations of significance also took place that afternoon and evening at Garvagh and Kilrea but in both cases the rebels decided they were not strong enough to defeat the nearby garrisons and dispersed.

Significantly there was little Catholic participation in the Antrim and Derry risings. Catholics and Anglicans had not joined in large numbers and Presbyterians formed the great mass of the rebels. But the United Irishmen had formed alliances with the Defenders in some areas and at Randalstown a large Defender contingent marched alongside the Presbyterians, albeit with a separate flag. Elsewhere the Catholic population, even if it had been marginally involved in the movement, remained aloof once the rising started. The first major republican movement in Ulster remained, from start to finish, essentially a Presbyterian phenomenon which Catholics largely chose to avoid.

As the day ended, the rebels had managed to take possession of most of Co. Antrim. However, they had not followed up their mobilisation in Derry with any military successes and they had failed disastrously to take Antrim town, the key to McCracken's strategy. At this point, General Nugent, the government commander in the North, had decided to keep his forces concentrated in and around Belfast and had sent out far fewer reinforcements than available towards the rebel-held areas. As a result, in spite of the dispersals that had already taken place, there was every chance that the Antrim rebels might soon regain the momentum and once again threaten Antrim town and even Belfast. From Nugent's perspective though, the fact that no rebellion broke out in Co. Down on 7 June was an important sign. By this time, the county's United Irishmen colonels

Henry Joy McCracken: an important figure in the Antrim United Irishmen from the outset. He led the more militant element which pushed for a Rising after the Leinster outbreak, and commanded the Antrim rebels at Donegore Hill and Antrim town. He was captured and executed after the movement collapsed.

had all been arrested along with William Steele Dickson, thus neutralising the United Irishmen there, at least for the time being.

In Dublin Castle, Camden and Lake were unaware of the day's developments in Antrim and Derry. Their attention was still focused on Wexford where for a second day in succession the rebels remained checkmated. Their forces at Carrickbyrne were still in a shattered condition and the officers at Gorey Hill were still frustrated and hesitant to take the initiative. During the evening, they finally broke camp and marched west to Carnew, preceded by a large cavalry patrol, and took possession of the town which had been evacuated by Loftus three days earlier. They set a large part of the town on fire and camped for the night on Kilcavan Hill, just to its north.

Meantime, in the south of the county some important changes took place in the command structure. Someone in Wexford town had sent word to Gorey that Edward Roche should come south and assume the position of commander-in-chief in place of Harvey while Fr Philip Roche, also an officer in the northern division, was to replace Harvey as commander of the Carrickbyrne division. Roche's task was evidently to coordinate the military effort since he now seems to have spent his time between Vinegar Hill and Wexford town. He promptly issued a proclamation calling on all Wexford people to fight in the name of liberty. This suggests that he no longer saw the Wexford rebels as part of the larger United Irishmen movement but rather as fighting alone; hence the more centralised command structure and the call to arms on behalf of an ideal worth fighting and dying for.

Friday, 8 June 1798

On 8 June the rebellion in Co. Antrim, in spite of its impressive successes the day before, began to unravel. General Nugent understood the situation of the rebels well. He published an amnesty for all rank-and-file rebels who turned in their weapons, promising that only the leaders would be court-martialled. This, in combination with the previous day's confusion, was enough to steal the initiative from McCracken. As the day passed, a second assault on Antrim town began to look less and less likely and by evening rebel camps all over the southern part of the county were paralysed by uncertainty and in some cases were even beginning to disintegrate.

Because of the lack of leadership, there was as yet no mobilisation of rebel units in other Ulster counties, including Down. A young Scottish merchant from Lisburn named Henry Munro and a Presbyterian schoolteacher from Newtownards named William Fox tried to organise a rising. They contacted many of the captains in the central and eastern part of the county and at least some of these were already planning on making their move the next day. In an ironic repetition of the rebellion in Leinster, therefore, the United Irishmen of one region were preparing to risk all in open rebellion just as the tide was turning against their comrades who had already risen in another.

Meanwhile, for the third day in succession, the rebel and government forces in and around Wexford town avoided action. For their part the rebels were attempting to rebuild in anticipation of the next battles while the various government garrisons around the county, remembering the lesson of Tubberneering: that their forces should not be split, resisted any temptation to mount an uncoordinated offensive. Johnson and his two thousand men, therefore, remained entrenched in New Ross where they had now been for three days. Ancram held his position at Newtownbarry and Loftus, with a substantial garrison at Tullow and a small outpost at Tinahely, guarded the broad pass out of the Wexford lowlands through southwest Wicklow. Needham was now the key link in the chain. There was a small garrison in Rathdrum, which guarded the routes into the heart of the Wicklow mountains, but his garrison at Arklow was by far the largest outside New Ross. During the day it was reinforced by troops moving down from Dublin so that, by evening, it too approached two thousand men. Furthermore, after more than a day of trenching, his men were very well protected against a rebel attack.

The rebels themselves were perplexed at this stage. The northern division, after burning Carnew the evening before, had spent the night on nearby Kilcavan Hill and marched back to Gorey Hill during the day. They finally received a small consignment of gunpowder and decided to attack Arklow the next morning. Earlier in the day, a heated debate took place between a faction led by Garret Byrne of Ballymanus, a leading south Wicklow rebel, which wanted to abandon conventional war in favour of a guerrilla struggle from the mountains, and another group, made up mostly of the Wexford officers, who resisted this idea and demanded that the conventional struggle continue. For the moment Byrne's idea was voted down. In the south of the county, Fr Philip Roche was trying desperately to revive the fortunes of the southern division. As a first step, he abandoned the camp at Carrickbyrne and marched his army, still probably consisting of several thousand men, to Slieve Coilte, about four miles south of New Ross and overlooking the Barrow estuary. His reasons for doing this are not clear but he may have been trying to intimidate the small garrison at Duncannon Fort or he may even have expected a French landing in the inlet. His move made no difference to the military situation and Johnson and his garrison continued to maintain their grip on the route into Munster at New Ross.

Saturday, 9 June 1798

On 9 June, two full weeks since the Battle of Oulart and seventeen days since the risings in Kildare and Meath, the Gorey Hill rebels attacked Arklow in what amounted to their final attempt to win a morale-boosting victory and to break out of their county. Had they succeeded, even at this late stage, they might still have posed a serious threat to Dublin itself. At the same moment, the Down rebels mobilised and began to take control of the northern and central part of their county. Had they succeeded over the next few days, they might have revived the Antrim rising and might even have managed to march on Dublin from the opposite direction. In spite of the fact that the tide was already flowing very much their way, therefore, the events of this and the next few days would prove critical for Dublin Castle.

The rebellion in Down began at Saintfield in the middle of the county, when a rebel column attacked the town and forced the small garrison to withdraw to Belfast. From there word of the rising spread rapidly to the rest of the eastern part of the county and by evening rebel detachments had taken possession of Newtownards which had also been abandoned by its garrison. Other rebel units had managed to mobilise in the Ards peninsula and had launched an attack, albeit

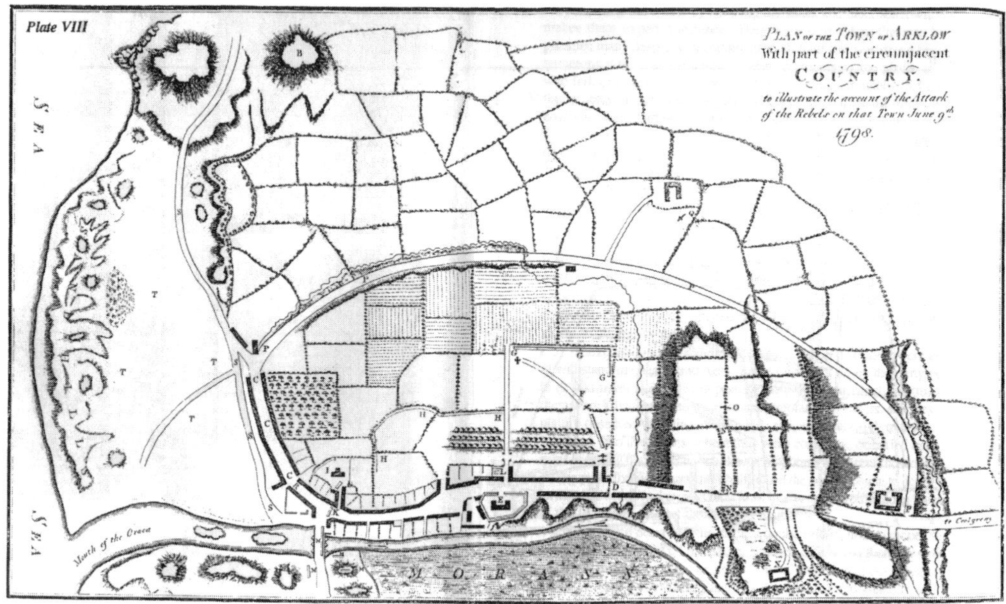

Arklow in 1798: the rebels attacked principally in the sectors marked D, F and G and also at the Fisheries, marked C. The present-day Catholic Church is located at D and the roundabout on the road to Gorey at A. (Musgrave)

unsuccessful, on Portaferry at its southern tip. As night fell, the rebel forces in Down were still rather scattered and uncoordinated but they had already taken possession of much of the northern and eastern part of the county. The government forces had offered little serious opposition to them anywhere, since Nugent was still anxious to keep a firm grip on the area around Belfast. Had the Antrim rebels not steadily dispersed during the day, the threat from Down would have looked much more formidable. As it was, it still amounted to a serious challenge to the northern commander, given that the Down insurgents would block his access to Dublin were they to succeed. At this stage, in fact, rebel units were indeed beginning to mobilise in the southern part of the county, expecting to join in the march on Dublin in the next few days.

In north Wexford the rebel army marched off Gorey Hill early in the day, making its way very slowly along the ten-mile route to Arklow and arriving in front of Needham's trenches and earthworks in the middle of the afternoon, the same time that their comrades in Co. Down were seizing Saintfield and spreading the word to rise in the parishes roundabout. The rebel officers opened their attack with a small artillery bombardment that did little damage and then they threw their forces simultaneously at the eastern and western ends of the town. The attackers did not make their way into the town itself, apart from some units that for a time threatened the bridge from the eastern entrance, but fierce fighting developed along the western and southern perimeter where Needham's men were well dug in. Several mass assaults on this part of the defences failed to break through. The battle ebbed to and fro for at least four or five hours and although at one point Needham seems to have been preparing for an evacuation the garrison held firm. At about eight o'clock the rebel officers called off the attack and ordered a retreat, which was orderly in most parts of the battlefront. However the garrison cavalry attacked rebels marching away from the eastern part of the town in some sandhills near the sea and cut down many. As night began to fall, at the very time that the Down rebels were consolidating their group on Saintfield and moving on Newtownards, the northern division of the Wexford rebel army was making its way back towards Gorey, not broken certainly but repulsed and badly damaged. They had failed to storm a vital town which they could have taken without opposition five days earlier and they had lost perhaps as many as five hundred men. The defeat was not quite so devastating as that at New Ross but the Gorey Hill division had never really tasted defeat up to this point, the small battle at Ballyminaun on 1 June being the only exception.

It is not surprising then that this was the last major offensive operation launched by either Wexford division. From this point on, the Wexfordmen would adopt a much more cautious and essentially defensive posture, waiting as they saw it to entice the government's forces to come and attack them. This was a sensible strategy in the circumstances but the government was already determined to play for time and to move when it suited them. For Camden and Lake, there were two conditions that needed to be fulfilled before they would eventually move against Wexford: rebellion had to be crushed elsewhere and reinforcements had to arrive from England. In the next three days the first of those conditions would be met and four days later so would the second.

The repulse at Arklow and the setback in Antrim had made it unlikely that the rebels could do much without help from somewhere. A small French expedition was preparing to sail to Ireland at this point and Wolfe Tone was to accompany it. However, it would not be ready for weeks yet and in the meantime Bonaparte had long since consigned his Irish strategy to the wastebin and was sailing with his fleet to Egypt. The reality was that whatever revolutionary forces in Ireland were to achieve they would have to achieve it alone.

CHAPTER 10

BALLYNAHINCH AND LIMERICK HILL

10 to 16 June 1798

The next week, beginning on Sunday 10 June, was to see the collapse of the Ulster rebellion while in Wexford the government forces and the rebels maintained an extraordinary stand-off, with neither side attempting a large-scale attack on the other. The Antrim rising was now over and the rebels in Co. Down were still scattered in several concentrations. On the first day of the week, rebel units in the eastern part of the county took possession of Bangor on the coast ten miles from Belfast, giving them control of most of the northeastern third of the county. Large numbers of insurgents flocked in and about seven thousand had gathered in the camp near Saintfield by nightfall. But they were now led by captains not colonels as the United Irishmen had not had time to replace those arrested the week before. This led to indecision and delay which ultimately cost them dearly. With a thousand men at Blaris and an even larger contingent in Belfast, Nugent was well-placed to go on the offensive whenever he chose.

The Wexford rebels were not in much better shape than the units in Co. Down. The Gorey Hill division was recovering from the previous day's disaster at Arklow and parties of stragglers were coming into the camp from morning until evening. Ten miles to the north, Needham's men were burying the hundreds of corpses they had found in the streets and fields roundabout but the commander refrained from any offensive action and merely sent cavalry patrols into the countryside to his south. He had been able to inform Dublin Castle of his success the day before, though, something which made the overall situation in the country look much more manageable to them.

The rebel division at Slieve Coilte, just south of New Ross, saw some action that morning when they attacked three gunboats moving down the Barrow estuary. They stopped one of the boats but the other two slipped past them and briefly bombarded Fethard village on the shore of the Hook peninsula. The bombardment did little damage but, ominously for the rebel leaders, the sound of the cannon could be heard across much of the southern part of the county in the quiet of that Sunday morning.

Monday, 11 June 1798

Next day the Co. Down rebels continued to consolidate their position. Henry Munro finally took charge of the Saintfield camp, which now included a large contingent of Defenders, and led the entire force to the village of Ballynahinch, about three miles to the southeast, where the local unit set up a new camp. With no sign of any reinforcements coming from Antrim, where they thought the rebellion might still be in progress, the Co. Down units were exhibiting extreme caution, of which Nugent and his forces were soon to take full advantage.

By this time the Wexford rebels began to realise their danger, hemmed into their own county as they were by government forces about whose real position and plans they were still confused. The garrison commanders at New Ross, Newtownbarry, Arklow and Tullow contented themselves with sending out small cavalry patrols to keep an eye on the rebel positions. During the day, the rebel leaders on Slieve Coilte broke camp and marched six miles due north to Lacken Hill, camping about two miles to the northeast of New Ross, which Fr Philip Roche was still planning to attack. That evening he sent a messenger to the smaller camp at Vinegar Hill asking for a detachment to join a column he intended to send out the following day to attack the small village of Borris, in south Carlow, to seize the arms and ammunition he needed for a successful attack on New Ross. Meanwhile, the rebel leaders in Wexford, fearing an attack by government naval forces, sent small detachments of troops out to Carne and Rastoonstown to watch the southern approaches to the harbour.

Tuesday, 12 June 1798

On Tuesday the Gorey Hill rebels moved their entire force northwards to Limerick Hill, two miles closer to Arklow and to the mountainous country on the south Wicklow border. A detachment of about three hundred men was sent to Aske Hill, two miles due east of Limerick Hill, to guard the right flank and the approach to Gorey. As they were doing this, the joint Vinegar Hill/Lacken Hill expedition to Borris, led by Thomas Cloney, marched without incident to the village. The attack on Borris House, the residence of a large Catholic landed family, the Kavanaghs, was met with stiff resistance from the local yeomanry and militia. The rebels attacked repeatedly but lost many men and eventually had to retreat back into Co. Wexford without gaining anything. Without the arms and ammunition he had hoped for, Fr Roche's chances of launching a successful attack on New Ross were now very slim. The government's strategy of containment, which they had maintained for eight days now, was making it next to impossible for the Wexford rebels even to learn what was happening in the rest of the country, much less to break out and join any other rebel forces that were in the field.

As for those other rebel forces in Co. Down, 12 June would turn out to be a fatal day. The forces massed at Ballynahinch were still dithering over their next move when General Nugent in Belfast suddenly took the initiative. He sent out small detachments to the village of Comber to cut off the rebels in the Ards peninsula from the main concentration at Ballynahinch. At the same time, he had his garrison in Downpatrick march on Ballynahinch from the south while he made his way at the head of about fifteen hundred men to attack from the north. Comber was taken easily and Nugent marched to Saintfield, which was now abandoned but which he had his men burn. As evening was coming on, he reached Ballynahinch and used his artillery to bombard the rebels' camp and the town until darkness began to fall. Then he decided to wait until dawn before continuing the attack.

The rebel force under Munro was now in a very vulnerable position. Although they outnumbered the government forces they had no artillery, were much more lightly armed and in a pitched battle were unlikely to have success. During the night hundreds of them deserted, including the contingent of Defenders, though Munro and his captains managed to keep several thousand men in the camp. That night they decided on a morning attack on the town itself, which lay just below their camp, with the intention of fighting Nugent to a standstill in the streets.

Early in the morning Munro sent a large detachment of rebel pikemen down into the town where they were immediately attacked by militia units. They fought them off and killed about thirty soldiers. In the next few hours, however, Nugent launched a fierce attack on the town and the countryside roundabout with his artillery and infantry. The rebels held out for a while but eventually began to retreat and the retreat quickly turned into rout. Nugent threw his cavalry mercilessly at the fleeing men. By mid-morning perhaps as many as four hundred lay dead in and about the town. Included among the dead was Betsy Gray, a young woman rebel, who would soon become a local legend. She died fighting beside her lover and her brother, shot by the yeomanry as they tried to escape. The rebel captains tried hard to rebuild their columns during the rest of the day but with no success. The rank-and-file drifted back to their homes to take advantage of Nugent's amnesty policy. The rising in Ulster was effectively over and by nightfall only the Wexford rebellion was still alive, even if the units there would not know for several days more that once again they were fighting completely alone.

In fact, the day of the battle of Ballynahinch passed quietly in Wexford. Patrols sent out towards Arklow from the camp on Limerick Hill, now the main

'A Typical Irish Insurgent': rebel officers were usually on horseback and carried swords and pistols – though not lances or pikes; the infantry in the background is portrayed as half-savage, typical of the loyalist view.

northern post, spotted some government patrols in the distance but Needham refused to be enticed into an attack and remained stubbornly behind his fortifications. Johnson did likewise at New Ross and Fr Philip Roche's force on Lacken Hill, deflated by the failure of the Borris expedition, had no choice but to stay where they were too. Desertions were becoming a problem and the once huge rebel army had shrunk now to a few thousand men.

Wednesday, 14 June 1798

On Wednesday 14 June the Ulster rebellion dissolved completely. Nugent's men were now busy looking for ringleaders and urging rebel units still under arms to abandon the cause and return home. They had considerable success as the day passed. In Co. Wexford the rebel cause continued to suffer from the frustrations forced upon it by Lake's strategy of containment and it also showed serious signs of internal tensions. At Lacken Hill Fr Philip Roche began to prepare for an assault on New Ross sometime later in the week though he must surely have realised there was little chance of success and may simply have been trying to stop desertions. These were a problem in the north of the county by now too: the detachment at Aske Hill had shrunk from around three hundred to about a hundred men. At Limerick Hill the officers, still unable to entice Needham to attack, sent a large detachment to Mountpleasant, a small hill almost ten miles into the mountains to the south of Tinahely. This may have been an attempt to convince the men that they were about to take an initiative of some sort.

The most significant developments of the day were taking place in and around Wexford town. A messenger from one of the garrisons in Wicklow arrived and indicated that the government wished to negotiate for Lord Kingsborough's release. Several of the rebel leaders used the opportunity to open the whole matter of a negotiated settlement. They sent a small delegation back northwards with a message for the government's commanders in Wicklow, suggesting they were willing to entertain such an approach. However, the mission was sabotaged when the delegation was halted at Vinegar Hill by a Captain Thomas Dixon, who seems at this point to have been emerging as the leader of a very militant faction in Wexford town. It was clear that rebel leaders like Harvey and Keogh realised that game was up but clearly there were also individuals like Dixon who wanted to fight on regardless.

In reality, the Wexford rebels' situation at this stage called for negotiation though they were not aware of developments. That very day Lake got word to his commanders in the midlands and Munster to converge on Wexford: Dundas, Eustace and Duff in the midlands and Brigadier-General John Moore in Cork all began to march towards the rebellious county. Once they got to the borders of Wexford the rebel leaders would be facing a government force of at least ten thousand men. Considering the number of desertions, the combined forces of the Wexford rebels may barely have exceeded that number and by now they were low on ammunition and serviceable firearms. With Bonaparte and his fleet getting further away in the Mediterranean every day, Tone's French invasion force still weeks from departure and the rebellion outside Wexford now completely crushed, the cause, in a military sense, was already irretrievably lost.

Thursday, 15 June 1798

On Thursday 15 June the situation in Wexford town deteriorated. Thomas Dixon and his growing group of militants initiated a serious internal power struggle against Matthew Keogh and the more moderate rebel leaders. Threats of violence forced Keogh to go into hiding. Outside the town, Fr Philip Roche encamped at Lacken seems to have persisted with his hopeless plan to attack New Ross and sent word across the southern half of the county calling on all able-bodied men to report to the camp. Only in the north of the county was there any significant change. During the afternoon, the Limerick Hill leaders decided to abandon camp for the second time in four days and to march their entire division out to Mountpleasant for an attack on Tinahely and its small garrison the following day. This would be only the third time in the rebellion that a large force of Wexford rebels would move outside the county. They were probably beginning to consider seriously the guerrilla 'mountain strategy' proposed earlier by Garret Byrne even though they were still, even at this late stage, unsure of what was taking place in the rest of the country.

CHAPTER 11

Lake's Foxhunt

16 to 22 June 1798

The government launched its campaign to crush the Wexford rebellion finally on Saturday 16 June, three weeks after the first rebel mobilisation in the county. Lake approached the challenge with great caution, even meticulousness, and in its early phases the invasion of the county and the effort to destroy the rebel forces was stunningly successful. In the end, however, a combination of Lake's short-sightedness and the rebels' skill and determination allowed the United Irishmen to survive the onslaught and to open an entirely new phase of the conflict.

The critical event of the day was the arrival of about a thousand British troops in Dublin. Three thousand more were known to be on the way. This allowed Lake to reinforce the Dublin garrison significantly and over the next day or two to redeploy the troopships along the Wexford coast. The preliminary moves against the rebellious county were already afoot. Duff and Dundas in the midlands were preparing to move south and Brigadier-General John Moore, later to become famous in the Peninsular War in Spain and to die at the siege of La Coruña, was moving eastwards from his normal station in Cork. He reached the town of Clonmel by evening and Lake's intention was to have him march all the way to New Ross over the next two days.

The rebels were not aware of these movements. The division at Limerick Hill spent the day marching across the hilly country to Mountpleasant and by evening was encamped above Tinahely and in a good position to overawe or overwhelm the small garrison below them. The Lacken camp saw no action and there were few signs that Fr Roche's plan to attack New Ross would go ahead. In Wexford town, the internal disputes intensified and at one point in the day Thomas Dixon and a handful of his followers barged into a room in which Matthew Keogh was holding a meeting. Dixon fired a shot at Keogh but missed and Keogh and the other more moderate leaders quickly bundled the Dixonites out of the building. This defused the threat for the moment but both sides must have realised that the internal struggle was far from over.

Sunday, 17 June 1798

Next day saw a few encouraging developments from the rebel perspective. At Tinahely the garrison's cavalry put up a short resistance which ended in the entire government force fleeing to Tullow and leaving the town to the rebels. They immediately set almost every building on fire. The column of smoke attracted hundreds of rebels who had been hiding in the hills and they joined the ranks. This was at least a military victory, the first since Tubberneering two weeks earlier. It might also have revived rebel hopes had it not been for the fact that the rebels who now joined them confirmed that the uprising in the midlands had been completely crushed. If Garret Byrne's mountain strategy was still being discussed (and it surely must have been at this point) the Tinahely victory was obviously an important first step in adopting it, especially since some of the new arrivals asserted that rumours of an imminent French landing were circulating in Dublin.

In Wexford town, too, there was at least one encouraging sign. During the day a highly disciplined detachment of rebels that had been sent out to Vinegar Hill a week earlier returned and imposed order on what was becoming a dangerous situation, thereby restoring Keogh's authority. The Dixonites were still far from finished but at least the more moderate rebels regained a position from which they might eventually be able to negotiate with the government.

The government, in the meantime, was beginning to close the jaws of the vice. Between morning and evening, Moore travelled from Clonmel to Waterford, where a messenger was awaiting him with orders to go on to New Ross the next day. Duff broke camp in Kildare and began a march towards Newtownbarry, Lake joined Dundas at Baltinglass and together they led Dundas's force south as far as Hacketstown by evening. By nightfall Lake had dispatched a messenger to Loftus in Tullow ordering him to make a rendezvous with the Hacketstown troops at Carnew the following morning.

Monday, 18 June 1798

Next day, the weather turned cloudy and cool. Normally this would have been unremarkable but it had been extraordinarily hot and dry for weeks up to this point, making life easier in the rebel camps and leading some of the simpler men and women among them to interpret the warm weather as a good omen. As the clouds rolled in over Ireland on 18 June, therefore, it would have been natural for such people to regard the change with foreboding.

During the day, Lake's strategy began to fall into place. Moore reached New Ross around midday, bringing the garrison up to about three thousand men and Duff's arrival in Newtownbarry increased the garrison there to two thousand. On the northwest borders of Wexford, government forces moved into position to attack the county also, but here matters were more complicated. The rebel division at Mountpleasant shifted camp southwards during the day to Kilcavan Hill, overlooking Carnew. It is not clear if they were aware of Lake's movements but when Lake and Dundas approached Carnew from Hacketstown and when Loftus advanced along the road from Tullow, they found the rebels in a strong position to block any further advance. Lake tried first to intimidate the rebel force into retreating and then sought to entice them to attack him in Carnew but the rebel leaders resisted both temptations. As night fell, Lake found himself in a quandary he had not expected: the rebel force on the hill was too large to attack but he could not afford to march on into Wexford and leave them in his rear.

In the end though, the rebel leaders played into Lake's hands. Seeing the convergence of government forces on the county, someone, possibly Edward Roche, decided to concentrate all the rebel forces at a central point and try to defeat the combined government forces in a field battle. Accordingly, a horseman arrived at the Kilcavan camp during the night with orders to retreat to Vinegar Hill. The northern officers were disappointed but complied and by dawn, to Lake's likely amazement, they were already several miles along the road to Gorey.

Tuesday, 19 June 1798

At the same time other government forces were on the move. On the morning of 19 June, Moore and Johnson in New Ross, Needham in Arklow and Loftus at Carnew marched into Co. Wexford in the first phase of Lake's invasion. It had begun to rain before dawn, slowing down the operation considerably, but the government troops made rapid progress and by afternoon had accomplished with remarkable ease everything Lake had hoped for. Needham and his force of almost two thousand men marched from Arklow to Gorey without meeting any opposition and Loftus and his men made their way from Carnew to the little bridge at Craanford, halfway to Gorey, without hindrance. Most striking of all, Moore and Johnson moved out of New Ross to see the rebel force camped on Lacken Hill melt away before their eyes and flee eastwards without putting up a fight. By evening Johnson had returned to New Ross, as Lake had ordered, in preparation for a march on Enniscorthy next day and Moore was camped at Foulkesmills after sweeping past the abandoned Carrickbyrne campsite. These were exactly the positions Lake had planned on occupying by the end of the day and the ease with which the northern and southwestern corners of the county had fallen to him must have surprised him. His plan was to close in on Enniscorthy and Wexford town the following day.

By now, the rebel leaders were reeling. Considering the caution of the goverment forces for weeks, Roche and the other officers could not have anticipated such a lightning attack and seem to have been caught unawares. The

Brigadier-General John Moore (later Major-General Sir John Moore), commander of the government forces at Lacken Hill, Goff's Bridge, Wexford town and Glenmalure. Known by both sides as a humane soldier, he died in the war against Bonaparte in Spain.

southern division spent the day retreating all the way eastwards as far as Wexford town, which they finally reached around midnight. The northern division, encumbered by thousands of refugees fleeing from the government soldiers and their atrocities, including many murders and rapes that first day of the invasion, managed to get only as far as Camolin by nightfall. In Wexford town crisis loomed. Battleships appeared off the harbour, a sign that the cause was hopeless. That night, Keogh and the officers of the old Lacken division held a hurried council of war and decided to pull together a new army which would march out the next morning and meet Moore in an open, last-ditch battle. As they did so, Thomas Dixon came into the town from the countryside to its immediate north at the head of a band of his followers who billeted themselves in the barracks for the night. He and his men seemed to have no plans to fight in the next day's battle. As it turned out, their designs were far more macabre than that.

Wednesday, 20 June 1798

Next day, Lake's plan continued to unfold as he had anticipated. Needham pushed south from Gorey and reached Oulart. Loftus and Dundas, with Lake himself directing the march, made their way southwards from Craanford and Carnew, halting by late afternoon at Solsborough Demesne, near Scarawalsh Bridge and the confluence of the Bann and Slaney Rivers. This placed them and their force of around three thousand men about two miles north of Enniscorthy where Duff joined them with his two thousand men. Meanwhile, Johnson marched from New Ross and was in place on the southwestern outskirts of Enniscorthy by sundown. All these marches were accomplished without appreciable resistance from rebel forces and by the end of the day, without having to fight a single action, Lake had trapped the rebels into the central and southern parts of the county

The northern division of the rebel forces had been helpless to stop this. They spent the day in renewed retreat, again hampered badly by refugees who took up a huge stretch of the road and it took them all day to make their way from Camolin to Vinegar Hill, where they finally arrived as night was falling. Most of the men, exhausted from two days of very difficult marching, immediately fell asleep.

The only area of the county where government forces faced serious resistance to their advance was in the south and here the resultant struggle turned out to be a close thing. During the morning, Moore had expected to be joined by a small detachment of British regulars at Foulkesmills, led by Lord Dalhousie. As the hours passed and Dalhousie did not arrive, he decided to break camp and march on to Taghmon, his destination for the day. A short distance into his journey, at a place called Goff's Bridge, he and his thousand or so men ran headlong into the rebel army of perhaps six thousand which had come out from Wexford town. In one of the fiercest battles of the war, the larger but poorly equipped rebel army, led by Fr Philip Roche, Thomas Cloney and John Henry Colclough, almost broke through Moore's lines. In the end, however, Moore fought them to a standstill and after several hours of fighting they withdrew, leaving several hundred men dead. Moore decided to camp for the night where he was and abandon the plan to reach Taghmon that night. This was the first setback to Lake's general plan but Moore was still in a strong position, especially since Dalhousie did finally join him that evening.

In Wexford town the rebellion, now in its final days, had taken an appalling turn. When the main rebel force under Roche, Cloney and Colclough was engaged in the Battle of Goff's Bridge, Thomas Dixon and his followers broke into the gaol and other buildings in which loyalist prisoners had been confined for weeks and hauled them out, a few at a time, to a hurried trial at the Custom House. Those found guilty of vague charges of crimes against the people – almost

Cruickshank's representation of the Wexford Bridge massacre: Prisoners were killed in this cruel fashion but Cruickshank's racism is obvious from the ape-like features of the rebels – in contrast to those of their victims.

all of them – were condemned to death. They were then marched off to the bridge where they were executed by pike thrusts and their bodies thrown into the river. In a few hours more than ninety men died in a chillingly brutal manner. The killing ended when Edward Roche appeared at the north end of the bridge to announce that Vinegar Hill was under threat and all should repair to defend it at once. Lord Kingsborough and a few score other prisoners had somehow managed to escape the bloodbath but this massacre, along with the killings at Scullabogue, put an end to any hope men like Keogh would have had of obtaining mercy from Lake.

Thursday, 21 June 1798

Next morning, Lake's own assault began. Just before dawn he attacked the rebel positions in Enniscorthy and on Vinegar Hill from the west and north. During the night, he had summoned Needham to join him from Oulart and Needham was now ordered to move around to the south of the rebel force to cut off their retreat. Over the next four or five hours a fierce battle developed in the town and along the slopes of the hill with government artillery and musketry taking a terrible toll of both rebels and refugees huddled in their thousands on the hillside. In the end the rebel army managed with considerable skill to extricate itself and retreated in fairly good order along the main road towards Wexford town. The refugees did not fare so well and hundreds of them were killed as they tried to escape.

Lake now had the victory he had wanted and had driven the rebel force south before him where they were bound to be trapped. He had, however, neglected one important detail. By summoning Needham to take part in the battle for Enniscorthy, he had left a gap, eight miles wide, between Vinegar Hill and the coast, a gap Needham would have closed off had he stayed at Oulart. To compound the mistake, Moore had resumed his march on Wexford town as the battle at Enniscorthy was going on, passing through Taghmon during the afternoon and pushing on towards Forth Mountain, long an important rebel camp. By this time, however, most of the rebels had left the camp and instead of holding the high ground thousands of them were milling about in the streets of Wexford. The two old rebel armies, the southern division that had once attacked New Ross and the northern one that had recently defended Vinegar Hill, now met again for the first time since the end of May. They were confused, trapped and desperate for an escape route. Some of their leaders had already given up. Bagenal Harvey and John Henry Colclough had slipped away with plans to hide out on the Saltee Islands, a few miles off the coast, and others, such as Matthew Keogh, had decided to throw themselves on the mercy of the government and were working frantically to negotiate a surrender. They sent Thomas Cloney and Edward Hay to Enniscorthy in the hope of persuading Lake to agree to terms of some kind. Lake spurned the approach so the rebel leaders now approached Lord Kingsborough to accept the formal surrender of the town to him.

Most of the more junior rebel colonels were uncertain of what to do though and as they hesitated they were told that a government army was approaching the town from the west. This was enough to spur them into action. They quickly split into two large columns, one under Fr John Murphy and Fr Philip Roche, the other under Anthony Perry, Edward Fitzgerald, and Edward Roche. The first group marched out of the town to the south and within a few hours had got cleanly away and camped for the night at Sleedagh Demesne, a few miles due south of Forth Mountain. The other column also escaped, marching more than ten miles northwards along the coast, and camped for the night at Peppard's Castle, about eight miles due east from Enniscorthy. That evening, Moore sent a small yeomanry party into Wexford to take possession of the town and release the remaining loyalist prisoners. Amazingly, however, neither he nor Lake realised that that one rebel army had slipped away to the south and another to the north where it was well positioned to get away from Lake's grasp altogether. The dragnet that Lake had pulled across the rebellious county may have had few if any holes. But it was pulled too tightly at either end and the rebel leaders were about to take their men completely around it. Lake would not realise for days what had happened and by then the rebel columns would be far away.

CHAPTER 12

THE SECOND WEXFORD RISING

22 June to 4 July 1798

On Friday 22 June, General Lake and his supporting officers converged on Wexford town and took possession of what had been the rebel capital. Immediately he ordered the arrest of all the rebel officers and officials he could find, ignoring the terms of the previous day's surrender to Lord Kingsborough. A 'White Terror' of a kind now began, with soldiers committing many atrocities, including murder and rape. But most of the rebel leaders were still missing and the vast majority of rebel rank-and-file were not to be found either, in spite of the publication of an amnesty for all but the leaders.

Meantime, the two rebel columns that had escaped Lake's clutches the day before were slipping further away from his grasp with each passing hour. The column that had camped at Peppard's Castle marched twenty-five miles to Croghan Mountain, on the northwestern border with Wicklow, by evening. On the way, they made a brief diversion into Gorey. At Coolgreaney, they attacked a body of loyalists fleeing from the town and killed about fifty of them in revenge for atrocities the yeomanry had committed in the area the day before. The other column, headed by Fr John Murphy, conducted an extraordinary march too, passing across the southwestern part of Wexford and camping in Scullogue Gap in the Blackstairs Mountains almost thirty miles from their overnight camp at Sleedagh.

Saturday, 23 June 1798

Next day, Lake commenced his liquidation of the rebel leadership in Wexford town by having John Hay, the brother of Edward Hay, tried and executed. Forty miles to the north, the rebels at Croghan broke camp and marched several miles into Wicklow and camped at Ballymanus, the home of Garret Byrne, while the column under Fr John Murphy swept down into Co. Carlow, crossed the Barrow at Goresbridge, where they defeated a small garrison that briefly opposed them, and then marched northwards through Kilkenny. They finally camped for the night a few miles from Castlecomer, well-known as a strong centre of the United Irishmen.

The capture of Bagenal Harvey, right, and John Henry Colclough, left, on the Saltee Islands. The representation is fairly accurate.

Sunday, 24 June 1798

On 24 June, Lake had several of the rebel leaders tried by military courts and sentenced to death. Among them were Matthew Keogh and Fr Philip Roche, who had left Fr John Murphy's column and slipped back into Wexford town two days earlier. Lake's men also discovered and arrested three prominent rebel officers, Bagenal Harvey, John Henry Colclough and Cornelius Grogan, a prominent landowner who had been the rebel commissar. All three would stand trial over the next two days.

The main rebel columns stayed on the move. That morning Fr Murphy's force, aided by coalminers who came out to join him, attacked Castlecomer and eventually took possession of the town in spite of strong opposition from the garrison. However, the battle was costly in casualties and yielded little by way of arms or ammunition. The other rebel column abandoned its camp at Ballymanus and marched westward with hopes of attacking Hacketstown, in northern Co. Carlow, and seizing the arms they so badly needed. At sundown they were within striking distance of the town but decided to wait for morning before launching an assault.

Monday, 25 June 1798

Next day, nine leading rebel officers, Keogh and Roche included, were hanged on Wexford Bridge. Lake was still focusing on the south of the county and what he thought were the remnants of the rebel army, unaware for the fourth day since Vinegar Hill that most of the rebels had eluded him. Fr Murphy's columns had, in fact, camped for the previous night just inside Queen's County. They had not attracted the recruits they had expected and, with pressure mounting on them from nearby garrisons, they conducted a forced march southwards towards the Blackstairs and Wexford once again. They got to Kilcumney Hill, a low hill in southern Carlow, by nightfall and stopped there until morning. Meantime, their comrades at Hacketstown launched a spirited attack on the garrison but met with equally strong resistance. By the afternoon, after losing at least a hundred men, they decided to pull back and spent the rest of the day and evening making their way back to their old camp at Croghan. Their strategy was obviously not working and had they not been waiting for other detachments, including Fr Murphy's, to join them they might have gone on into the mountains at this point.

Tuesday, 26 June 1798

Tuesday proved a fateful day for Fr Murphy and his column. They had successfully marched an immense distance since leaving Wexford town and had fought off all efforts to stop them. Just after dawn, however, they were surprised by government forces attacking from three sides and retreated hastily across southern Carlow towards the mountains. During the retreat Fr Murphy became separated from his men and was captured several days later. The column was demoralised and most of the men elected to give up the struggle and return to their homes. A remnant decided to push northwards towards the border with Wicklow and set out across country, led by Miles Byrne, an eighteen-year-old rebel officer and a cousin of Garret Byrne. They were aiming to join the Croghan force which had spent the day in the safety of their camp recovering from their defeat at Hacketstown. Their main concern was to encourage straggling units to catch up with them before they pushed on into the mountains, but up to then few had arrived.

Lake's liquidation of the rebel leaders who were in his grasp continued on this, the fifth day since he entered Wexford and he now put Cornelius Grogan on trial. Grogan defended himself well and by evening the process was still not completed but Lake was determined to have his revenge and there must have been an air of inevitability about the proceedings, in spite of Grogan's brave stand.

General John Moore, second from left on horse, recaptures Wexford from the rebels: an English impression of the battle.

Wednesday, 27 June 1798

Next day the trial was resumed and Grogan was found guilty that afternoon. Bagenal Harvey was also tried with the same result, both men being condemned to hang the next day. General Hunter, who had been stationed in the Channel Islands, arrived in Wexford to assume command in the county, freeing Lake to take ship for Dublin that afternoon to coordinate the resistance to a French invasion, should one still come. Meantime, the rebels at Croghan remained in their camp, still waiting for stragglers to join them as the little force under Miles Byrne picked its way painstakingly across the northern parishes of Wexford.

Thursday, 28 June 1798

On Thursday the rebel force at Croghan continued stubbornly to hold its ground. Fitzgerald, Perry, Edward Roche and the other officers in the camp seem to have been aware that several other important colonels, including Fr Mogue Kearns, Fr John Murphy and Thomas Cloney, were alive and waiting to join them at some point soon. Otherwise, their hesitation in escaping to the security of the Wicklow mountains is impossible to explain.

General Hunter, now in command in Wexford, continued Lake's trials and executions, having Grogan, Harvey and another prominent rebel, Patrick Prendergast, hanged on the bridge. During the afternoon, John Henry Colclough was tried and was hanged before sundown. Hunter also began a significant redeployment of his troops, evidence that he realised the rebellion was not over. He ordered Moore to Taghmon and sent Johnson back to his original post in Cork. He had Duff move northwards to Newtownbarry, ordered Needham to move up to Gorey and sent Colonel Grose, one of his own officers, to establish a strong garrison at Enniscorthy, with a small outpost at Ferns. The Arklow garrison, small since Needham left, received some reinforcements from Dublin at this point too, putting the government forces in a good position to go on the offensive in the hill country along the Wexford/Wicklow border.

Friday, 29 June 1798

Next day there were no new developments, in spite of the fact that Needham in Gorey and Duff in Newtownbarry were now well aware of the rebel presence to their north. The rebel officers, in the meantime, making decisions by committee, kept their little army in camp, still evidently hoping against hope that men like Cloney, Kearns and Murphy might yet arrive.

Saturday, 30 June 1798

Finally on Saturday the stalemate was broken. Under cover of darkness, Needham sent out from Gorey a cavalry patrol, led by a notorious local yeoman named Hunter Gowan, to reconnoitre the rebel camp. Gowan returned by dawn with news that the rebel force was encamped at the foot of Croghan and might be overwhelmed in a surprise attack. A few hours later, however, Needham got word that the rebels had suddenly broken camp and were marching in the direction of Carnew. He sent a large cavalry detachment out to harass them as they marched. When the rebel leaders discovered that the cavalry was approaching they set up a perfectly planned ambush at Ballyellis, on the Gorey/Carnew road near the border with Wicklow. The cavalry was devastated in the attack that followed and the survivors fled back to Gorey in complete disarray. The rebels pressed on to seize what arms they could in Carnew and by evening had established a camp at Kilcavan Hill, the third time in the rebellion they had used this site. Compared with some of the previous battles, the encounter at Ballyellis was small but it was an important victory for the rebels and may have persuaded them to stay near the border for a few more days and give their comrades to the south yet another chance to join them.

Sunday, 1 July to Wednesday, 4 July 1798

Over the first four days of July, the rebel army continued to stay close to the Wexford/Wicklow border but was clearly preparing to make the long-delayed journey into the mountains. On Sunday 1 July they remained at Kilcavan all day and next day marched westwards across the barony of Shillelagh and fought an

Father Murphy on Vinegar Hill: he was on the Hill on the day of the battle and played a prominent role, though not perhaps quite so prominent as this illustration suggests.

intensive and successful battle against a yeomanry force at Ballraheen Hill. Fifty of the yeomen were killed and the rebels got some valuable guns and ammunition, though far less than they needed. That night, after an unsuccessful attack for more weapons on a large and well-fortified farmhouse, they moved eastwards again and camped once more at their old base, the White Heaps at the foot of Croghan.

On Tuesday, Miles Byrne and the remnant of Fr John Murphy's column finally joined them. Any doubts the leaders had about Murphy's continued involvement were now answered. That evening Garret Byrne and Edward Fitzgerald left the camp on horseback for a long and dangerous ride to Killoughram woods, in western Wexford, where they thought other units, led by Thomas Cloney and Fr Mogue Kearns, were hiding out. They were making sure that all who wanted to join them had done so before finally leaving the county.

The main body at Croghan passed the following day quietly, waiting for Byrne and Fitzgerald to return and preparing for the march into Wicklow. Sometime during the day Anthony Perry made his way back to his home near Inch to say a last farewell and a small rebel detachment destroyed a cluster of wooden huts built on the northern slope of Croghan during a small gold rush several years before. Anything that might be of use to the government in the weeks and months ahead was evidently to be denied them.

That night Fitzgerald and Byrne returned with Mogue Kearns but without Thomas Cloney who had decided to take his chances near his family and to withdraw from the struggle. Kearns, however, was determined to battle on and when he came into the camp several hours before dawn almost the entire northern Wexford and southern Wicklow United Irishmen leadership was reunited for the next stage in the war. Word was passed quickly through the camp that they would march at first light and finally, two weeks after Vinegar Hill, they were now ready to leave Wexford behind and carry on the fight elsewhere.

What the rebel officers did not realise at this point was that, a few days before, Lake had become well aware of their location and strength and Needham was preparing a four-pronged attack on Croghan within a few hours. The plan was for Needham himself to attack the rebel position from Gorey. The Marquess of Huntly, commander of a Highland regiment stationed in Arklow, would attack from the north across Croghan itself. Duff would march in from the west and a small detachment of troops would move up from Ferns to cut off any escape to the south. As they waited for the dawn, the rebel leaders were completely unaware that government forces were moving in to surround them. Equally, the government commanders had no idea of the rebels' intentions.

CHAPTER 13

THE LONG MARCH TO ULSTER

5 to 14 July 1798

On the morning of 5 July, the surviving Wexford United Irishmen embarked on an extraordinary undertaking which, over a ten day period, would see them finally leave their own county, move into the safety of the Wicklow mountains and then, for reasons that are still not clear, make a bold and desperate attempt to march all the way to eastern Ulster to join their Presbyterian comrades (see map page 36). In many ways, the decisions they made in these last ten days of their struggle would be the most puzzling of their entire rebellion.

The adventure began in dramatic fashion. At dawn on the first day, the Croghan army broke camp and began to march north-westwards towards the Wicklow Gap, a pass through the mountains into Co. Wicklow, about two miles from the White Heaps. To their complete surprise they marched headlong into James Duff's force of a thousand or so troops advancing directly against them. They retreated southwards for a few miles but turned and fought a fierce battle in the fields of a townland called Ballygullen, just north of the village of Craanford, which ended in stalemate after considerable losses on both sides. By then the three other government forces were converging on the rebel army which now split into two columns. A small detachment, led by Miles Byrne, slipped off to the west and hid in the hills near Carnew while the main body retreated southwards all the way to Carrigrew, almost twenty miles from Croghan. Large numbers of men were discouraged at this turn of events and left the column to make their way home, though most were determined to fight on. That evening, after they had recovered from the earlier ordeal, these men marched northwards again, avoiding the various government columns in northern Wexford and eventually slipping across the border into Co. Wicklow where they camped several miles into the Wicklow hills. The small detachment that included Miles Byrne never managed to catch up with them and over the next few days this group made its way into Glenmalure where it joined a number of Wicklow rebels, including the famous Michael Dwyer.

Joseph Holt, the Wicklow rebel officer, probably a good likeness: Holt was a skilled leader and dedicated rebel.

Friday, 6 July to Sunday, 8 July 1798

Next day, the main body, numbering around a thousand men, marched northwards into the heart of Co. Wicklow. They passed by Ballymanus, their campsite of 23 June, which had been burned to the ground since then and camped somewhere near Hollywood for the night. For the time being, government troops were not trying to penetrate the mountains so they faced little or no opposition.

The movements of the rebel column over the next two days are not clear but by the evening of 8 July they were camped at Borleas Demesne, outside Blessington. At this point, they had evidently made an extraordinary decision. Instead of following Garret Byrne's preference for carrying on a guerrilla war from the sanctuary of the mountains and waiting for a French landing, the leaders decided to march across the midlands, link up with the rebels at Timahoe and then make their way to Co. Down to join the Presbyterian United Irishmen. Either they thought the Presbyterian rebels were still holding out or they believed their own arrival would stimulate the northerners to rise again and build a springboard for a new rebellion, with or without French help. Garret Byrne is unlikely to have supported this move and Michael Dwyer appears to have backed away from it and left the column altogether; hence his presence in Glenmalure when Miles Byrne and his company got there. However, men like Edward Roche, Edward Fitzgerald, Anthony Perry and Fr Mogue Kearns may have supported the idea. Certainly it represented the same preference for conventional tactics that they seem to have insisted on time and again during the Wexford phase of the struggle.

As coincidence would have it, on this same day, 8 July, General Lake had made his way south to Arklow to coordinate an offensive against the rebel forces he now knew to be hiding out in the mountains. He ordered Needham to move to Rathdrum and Moore to march northwards through Enniscorthy and Carnew and to sweep into the Wicklow mountains through their western approaches. The plan was a sound one and could be accomplished, he expected, over the next five or six days. He was not aware, of course, that once again, just as he was about to close in on the rebels, they were about to change their whereabouts completely.

Monday, 9 July 1798

On 9 July, the rebel column, enlarged by recruits from Wicklow so that it may have numbered closer to two thousand men, set out across the plains of Kildare intending to join up with the rebel remnant at Timahoe. They marched past Kilcullen, avoided the larger garrison at Naas and camped in the central part of the county that night, having met no opposition except a small patrol which they overcame and from which they captured a valuable barrel of gunpowder. If they expected to gain more recruits from the central part of Kildare, once such a hotbed of the United Irishmen movement, they were bitterly disappointed. The rebel movement here was long since dead and there was little response from the local population to their passing.

In the meantime, Lake was pursuing his own plans. He moved down to Ferns during the day and Moore got as far as Enniscorthy. Lake's plan was that they should combine their forces the following day and make their way to Carnew; from there they would be within striking distance of what he thought was the main rebel campsite. The government forces marched without notable incident but once in Enniscorthy Moore took time to inspect the ravaged town and to climb to the top of Vinegar Hill, which still reeked of rotting corpses buried in its shallow soil. Moore, one of the few humane government commanders involved in the war, was shocked by what he saw and duly recorded his dismay in his diary that night.

Tuesday, 10 July 1798

The rebel column spent the day of 10 July marching northwards through Kildare, still trying to avoid contact with any substantial garrison and seeking out the Timahoe force. They finally encountered some of these men at

Prosperous, scene of one of the few rebel victories on the very first night of the Rising, and these led them into the fastness of the great bog where they met the Kildaremen's leader, William Aylmer. He convinced them to swing to the west the next day and attack the small garrison at Clonard, where there were arms stored, before pushing on to Ulster.

Lake and Moore were still making steady progress in their march. They met that morning in Ferns and marched together as planned to Carnew. There they stopped for the night and Moore got a chance to view yet another town that had been fought over several times and in which practically every house was now a burnt-out shell.

Wednesday, 11 July 1798

On Saturday, the combined Kildare, Wexford and Wicklow rebel force marched out of Timahoe and attacked Clonard. The garrison was small but well-armed, well-positioned and resolute. The insurgents launched a number of determined assaults on the buildings in which the soldiers were taking cover but could not dislodge them. By now, it was a familiar story, repeated so often in the rebellion: rebels armed with pikes and a few muskets found it impossible to storm strong stone buildings held by men who were better armed, albeit badly outnumbered. After several hours, the rebel officers called off the attack and the entire force retreated south-eastwards to the Hill of Carbury, where they camped for the night. It was a bitter and costly disappointment since their losses were very heavy. That night a dispute broke out among them on the wisdom of the march to Ulster and a number of men, including Joseph Holt, a famous Wicklow rebel, left the camp for the safety of the mountains. The rest of the force, now made up mostly of Wexfordmen and Kildaremen, decided to risk all next day in a march straight for Ulster. This route would take them through the regions of northern Kildare and southern Meath where the United Irishmen had been so strong at the outset. It was as if the Wexford rebel officers were determined to make one last swing through the heartland of the movement, in both Leinster and Ulster, before giving up the cause.

Lake and Moore had by now begun to close in on what they thought was the rebel stronghold in the Wicklow mountains. They marched out of Carnew early in the day, as the rebels were preparing at Timahoe for their attack on Clonard. By midday they reached Hacketstown and moved on that afternoon to a gap in the mountains leading into the series of glens in which they expected to find the rebel force. With Needham ready at Rathdrum to reinforce him should he require it, Lake finalised his plan for the assault. He decided to take up position himself at the village of Greenane, which guarded the mouth of the glen, while Moore would cross over its rim and come straight down at the rebels. Other government

Michael Dwyer, Wicklow rebel officer: he was involved in some of the fighting in Wexford but later led a band in the mountains and held out until 1803. Transported to New South Wales he eventually became a magistrate there. He died and was buried in Sydney.

forces from northern Wicklow were ordered to seal off escape routes to the north. At this stage the commander-in-chief could be forgiven for assuming that he was now on the point of completing the task he failed to finish in Wexford three weeks earlier.

Thursday, 12 July 1798

On 12 July, the rebels in Kildare began their march to Ulster. They decamped early in the day and marched along quiet country roads towards the northeast, heading straight for the rebel heartland of southern Meath. They saw no sign of government forces for several hours and covered the ground rapidly, riding on horseback now, mostly two men to a horse. They stopped at a place called Rynville to eat some of the provisions they still had and there noticed a government cavalry detachment following them. The cavalry was from Edenderry and kept behind them for the rest of the day. No other government forces put in an appearance and the rebels stopped near Dunboyne to camp for the night while the Edenderry cavalry pulled back and disappeared. During the night word of the rebels' whereabouts reached garrison commanders in Dublin, Navan and Drogheda, where there were large numbers of troops and from which an effective effort might be made to block their passage northwards. The rebels were disappointed by the refusal of the southern Meath men to join them and by the decision of most of the Kildaremen who had joined them to withdraw at this point. From now on the small rebel army was almost exclusively a Wexford force.

Lake and Moore had spent a frustrating day looking for the rebel force in the mountains of Wicklow. Moore had encountered heavy rain as he led his men across the rim of the glen and down into its bottom only to find no sign of the reported rebel camp. Most of the government forces were now in this part of Wicklow. By evening, however, they were ordered to converge on Blackmoor Hill, where the rebels were now said to have encamped, but these reports turned out to be false too.

Friday, 13 July 1798

On Friday, the extraordinary march of the rebel army continued. By midday they had reached Garristown Hill, just inside northern Co. Dublin, and by evening they had got as far as Co. Louth. They selected a spot for a campsite and rested until dawn, now within a day's travel of the Ulster border and the south Down countryside in which there had indeed been a strong United Irishmen movement. Lake and Moore were still in western Wicklow, attempting to discover where the rebels had disappeared to. Several other government commanders though had realised what was happening and were beginning to converge from several directions on the rebels on the Meath/Louth border. These included General Meyers from Dublin, General Meyrick from Navan and General Wemys from Drogheda. During the day, Meyrick and Wemys had tried to cut off the rebels before they got to the Boyne at Duleek but reached their rendezvous point too late and the rebels slipped over the river without ever realising how close they had come to being trapped. By nightfall, however, as the rebels settled in their camp, both generals moved up to within a mile or so of them and waited until morning before mounting an attack. The government force consisted of about a thousand men and by this stage probably outnumbered the exhausted, ragged and hungry rebels. They held off from a night attack though, evidently fearful of the reputation the Wexford rebels now had.

Friday, 14 July 1798

Next morning, 14 July – the ninth anniversary of the storming of the Bastille – the rebels resumed their march early, with the government's cavalry units harassing them from the rear. For a time the rebel officers tried to keep up the pace they were setting, hoping that the enemy would pull back or be held off. However, the attacks persisted and were eventually doing so much damage that Byrne, Roche, Kearns, Perry and Fitzgerald ordered the entire column to dismount and face about to draw their pursuers into a pitched battle. They chose a small causeway across a bog in a townland called Knightstown, which was ideally suited to the task. Instead of charging them as expected, however, the government cavalry simply held off and waited for their own main body of infantry, along with several pieces of artillery, to come up. When these were in place, Wemys and Meyrick launched a devastating cannonade and a musketry attack. The rebels tried to retreat across the bog to escape from the blistering fire but most of them lost formation and the battle turned into a near-rout.

When the rebels finally broke out into the open country beyond the bog a number of small detachments had become completely separated from the rest and slipped off towards the northwest and east. A fairly sizeable unit, numbering around three or four hundred men, led by Edward Fitzgerald, Edward Roche and Garret Byrne, managed to reassemble and turn south, abandoning hope of getting to Ulster and making instead for the Wicklow mountains, about fifty miles away. They still had their horses so that they had some chance of making the journey. A column of government soldiers moving over from Malahide encountered them at Garristown and began to follow and harass them. Eventually, at a place called Ballyboghill, Fitzgerald ordered his men to dismount and fight a last stand in a field that sloped up from a crossroads. Whether this move was absolutely necessary is unclear but its gallantry was certainly in keeping with the approach that many of the rebel commanders had maintained through much of the conflict. When the mounted government force charged them the rebels broke and fled. Most of them escaped somehow but they now lost all formation and scattered over the Dublin countryside. Scores of them managed to slip away once darkness fell and at least some of them managed to cover the distance to the mountains on foot over the next few days. These included Byrne and Fitzgerald but Perry and Kearns, who had become separated from the main body after Knightstown, were captured in Kildare and hanged at Edenderry a few days later. Whatever form the struggle was to take in future, all hope of a conventional struggle in either Ulster or Leinster was now, once and for all, completely gone. Only guerrilla warfare from the Wicklow mountains and/or a French landing could now sustain the movement.

CHAPTER 14

THE DEFEATED

15 July to 22 August 1798

Over the next four weeks, the Dublin civil and military authorities set about restoring what they regarded as order in the areas that had been affected by the rising. This involved a combination of policies, ranging from the conciliatory approach of John Moore, backed to a certain degree by some elements in Dublin Castle, to the vengeful approach of ultra-loyalists in every part of the country, with their backers in the capital urging them on and fighting an intense power struggle against the conciliationists. Meanwhile, as these policies unfolded and the battles over them mounted in intensity, the French army, the one element that everyone had assumed would be directly involved in the Irish war sooner or later, was finally getting ready to step in.

On 22 June, the day that the two Wexford rebel columns slipped past Lake's dragnet in Wexford and made their way to the Blackstairs and Croghan Mountains, Earl Camden had sailed out of Dublin for England. After three years he was being replaced as Viceroy by Lord Cornwallis, who had surrendered to George Washington at Yorktown in 1781 and who had since had a distinguished career in, among other places, India. William Pitt, the English Prime Minister, had decided weeks earlier to make this change and had it happened sooner it might have altered the course of events since Cornwallis was much more moderate in his politics and in his approach to war. The new Viceroy had not had time to settle into his post when the last phase of the Wexford rebellion was played out in Kildare and Meath but by 15 July, when it became obvious that the open war was over, he was in a good position to stamp his authority on the situation.

And his authority was certainly needed, for in Wexford, Down and Antrim, even more so than in the midlands, the campaign of retribution that began at the moment of the government victory had been continued with undiminished intensity ever since. For three weeks the country people of Wexford, whether former rebels long since returned to their homes (of which there were thousands) or completely innocent people, had been the victims of several outbreaks of rapine, murder and arson that had left parts of the region even more devastated than had the war itself. Particularly disturbing was the fact that arson attacks on Catholic chapels began to occur. This, in combination with the series of highly public executions of leading rebel officers, fed a general panic. A rumour spread across the county that loyalists planned to exterminate the entire Catholic population of certain districts, in particular the Macamores, the area running along the eastern coast of north Co. Wexford. The same sort of paranoia, typical enough of rural societies in the pre-modern age, also affected the Protestant population and rumours abounded of rebel bands hiding in various remote places in preparation for a massacre of Protestants. On several occasions these panics caused large numbers of Protestants in rural areas to take refuge in nearby towns. These waves of hysteria occurred all through the summer and even lasted into the following autumn and winter. Irrational fears undoubtedly kept many former rebels in hiding and stirred men like Hunter Gowan, the notorious leader of a yeomanry corps called the 'Black Mob', to fearsome depredations. Most ironically, they opened a gulf between the Protestant and Catholic communities in Wexford that was much wider than in the generation before the rebellion, a development that ran exactly counter to what the Wexford United Irishmen had planned in their new order.

In Ulster the loyalist retribution was merciless too. Because the rebels were almost all Presbyterians, the element of sectarian paranoia was absent there, as was much of the rapine and arson that took place in Wexford. However, large numbers of rebel officers were rounded up in the weeks following Ballynahinch and scores of them, even more than in Wexford, were hurriedly tried and hanged. While the loyalist retribution in Ulster took a different form than it did in South Leinster, therefore, it was in many ways just as brutal.

One of the first acts of the new Viceroy, taken while the rebellion was still going on, was to direct Lake and the other commanders to offer a general and unconditional amnesty and a guarantee of safety to the rebel rank and file. On 17 July, the day that Henry Joy McCracken was hanged, Cornwallis formalised this offer and three days later had parliament pass an Amnesty Act to copperfasten it. In counties like Wexford, Carlow, Antrim and Down, rebel bands in hiding were slow to trust the government. By the end of the month, few of them, especially in Wexford and Carlow, had taken advantage of the offer. Over the next few weeks, however, the response became stronger and, in spite of continued harassment by yeomanry and militia, hundreds at first and then thousands surrendered and went back to their homes equipped with the slip of paper that was their 'protection'. Some were unfortunate enough to fall victim to the vengefulness of local loyalists who took the protection itself as proof of involvement but by the middle of August most were rebuilding burnt-down houses and preparing to reap the harvest. By the end of the month, with the exception of Wicklow, where sizeable bands under the leadership of Michael Dwyer and Joseph Holt were still holding out, all of Leinster had become quiet.

For the prominent rebels, however, the captains, colonels and adjutant-generals, the weeks between mid-July and mid-August were less comforting. Once Cornwallis's hand began to be felt in military affairs the risk of mass executions, such as those that had seen so many rebel officers die in Ulster and Wexford, diminished. By the time that had happened, only Garret Byrne, Edward Fitzgerald, Thomas Cloney, Edward Hay and Edward Roche out of the Wexford officer corps of a dozen or so people, had survived. The rebel colonels in places like Carlow, Antrim and Down, where the pre-Cornwallis regime had had more time to operate, fared even less well. By the end of the summer though, Byrne, Fitzgerald, Cloney and Roche, as well as the Kildare rebel William Aylmer, had all surrendered to the government, encouraged by Cornwallis's obvious desire to end the bloodletting.

Most dramatic of all in this process was the fate of the eighty or so rebels who had been arrested in Dublin in the late spring and early summer, including those picked up in the raid on the home of Oliver Bond. Among them were some of the most important leaders of the United Irish movement. In the week after the final battle at Ballyboghill the government began to put the more prominent on trial. By 26 July, they had tried and executed the Sheares brothers, Oliver Bond, William Byrne, the Wicklow delegate arrested at Bond's, and John McCann, a leading member of the Leinster Directory.

Following the rash of executions, however, the rest of the prisoners negotiated an extraordinary agreement with the government. Most of them signed a letter promising to reveal all the details of their conspiracy, including their contacts with France, in exchange for clemency. The Irish House of Commons had already initiated a secret committee of inquiry into the United Irishmen movement and, when the government responded positively to their offer, the prisoners drew up a forty-page document outlining their organisational structure, giving information on their extensive contacts with France and plans for a French invasion, as well as details of their intention to create a democratic republic once they had succeeded. If there had been any doubt in the establishment's collective mind that they were dealing with a Jacobin-like movement, this dispelled it.

Within the establishment though, there was divided counsel at this point. Some, such as Cornwallis himself and even Lord Clare, the Lord Chancellor and long a proponent of severe measures, favoured a conciliatory policy and they were now having their way. Others still wanted revenge and severe retribution against a population a large part of which they regarded as implacably hostile. Unknown to many, Cornwallis and Clare were both aware of William Pitt's long-term plan to

William Samson: an early member of the United Irishman and among those arrested in Dublin shortly before the Rising. He was one of those pardoned as part of Cornwallis's agreement with prisoners.

have the Irish parliament eventually vote for constitutional union with Britain and so were conscious of the need to placate as many as possible of the leading Protestants, the people who would have to approve such a union. Cornwallis also wanted to continue to court the Catholic establishment which clearly abhorred the rebels and which would possibly benefit from the union with Britain by having its wealthier members be given the right to sit in Westminster. In the circumstances Cornwallis had to tread lightly in all directions.

The great imponderable, as it had been for months, was still the French. Britain was still alone in her struggle against the foreign revolutionary power that had inspired the rebellion in Ireland. To Cornwallis the end of the Irish rebellion appeared as just the end of a phase in a much larger struggle which might conceivably be renewed, perhaps even on Irish soil, in the coming months or years.

One county that might still be key to Ireland's response to a French landing

John Philpot Curran: member of a noted Irish Whig family and briefly suspected (along with Henry Grattan) of involvement in the United Irishmen. A brilliant lawyer, he defended the Sheares brothers and Wolfe Tone. He later opposed the Union but was reconciled to the change and took the office of Master of the Rolls.

was Wicklow. Here on 15 July sizeable rebel bands were still in existence, including the group of which Michael Dwyer and Miles Byrne were members and which had eluded Moore's and Lake's first incursion into the glens. Despite the rebels' escape, the enthusiasm of many of them for the cause waned steadily in the following four weeks. A critical factor was that Moore, who was increasingly directing the government's effort, managed to convince large numbers of the population in general and of their rebel relatives and friends that the amnesty was real. The result was that by the middle of August the guerrilla bands had dwindled in size. Although this made the remaining handful more mobile and so less easy to corner, it also meant that they were less of a potential threat should a French landing occur.

In France, these four weeks turned out to be critical. At this point, French troops were fighting, or preparing to fight, on three fronts. The first front was Egypt. After landing on Malta on 9 June, the day of the Battle of Arklow, Bonaparte spent the next four days taking control of the island. He spent the following three weeks sailing eastwards across the Mediterranean, landing in Egypt on 2 July and storming the city of Alexandria. Twenty days later, on 21 July, he defeated a native army at the Battle of the Pyramids. On 1 August, however, his fleet was suddenly attacked and almost annihilated by Admiral Nelson in what became known as the Battle of the Nile. In contrast to this stunning drama, the French forces on the second front, in Switzerland, were fighting their tedious war against the Alpine Catholic communities. The third front, or at least potential front, was Ireland and here, as well as in Egypt, the fortunes of France began to decline for the first time in several years.

In spite of Bonaparte's loss of interest, the French government had continued to plan for at least a small expedition to Ireland and the United Irishmen delegates, Wolfe Tone and Edward Lewins, had worked tirelessly to ensure that this in fact took place. By 14 July, they were planning to launch two separate expeditions, one to sail from La Rochelle under General Humbert, an old comrade of Hoche and a veteran of the failed Bantry Bay expedition, and the other from Dunkirk. Each force would consist of about four thousand men and would carry extra arms and ammunition to distribute to the Irish rebels. The plan called for Humbert to lead what amounted to an advance party of about a thousand men and for General Hardy to sail shortly after from Brest with the other three thousand. The Dunkirk force was to sail later as a follow-up. The French planners envisaged that Humbert and Hardy would land in northwest Ireland so as to get their forces ashore without opposition and expected that they could later link up with Irish rebels elsewhere and overwhelm the government forces. Wolfe Tone was to sail with the main force under Hardy. News of some sort of uprising in Ireland began to filter into the Low Countries and France during the month of June but even as late as the end of July there was still great confusion in Brest about what exactly was afoot. For Tone, however, as he waited in Brest for the preparations to be completed, the chances of success must have seemed considerable.

Other United Irishmen agents besides Tone and Lewins had been active for some time in France and they too were involved to one degree or other in these plans. They included Charles Teeling, an Ulster Catholic, and Napper Tandy, a member of the original Dublin society and a well-known radical from the 1780s.

There were a number of squabbles among these men but by the end of July it seemed that the French government was prepared to place at least some trust in them and their movement.

In early August, however, with the rebellion in Ireland now effectively over, the expeditions were beset by a succession of problems. The French government had been slow in paying the troops assigned to the invasion of Ireland. The thousand or so men waiting at La Rochelle were restive and the three thousand with Hardy and Tone at Brest were practically rebellious over this. On 6 August though, in spite of misgivings among his men, Humbert set sail, heading far out into the Atlantic with the intention of turning back towards the west coast of Ireland. By this point the crisis about money at Brest had reached boiling point and Hardy was unable to put to sea in support of Humbert. Sixteen days later, on 22 August, Humbert and his small fleet approached the coast of Mayo in Ireland. Instead of being a few days behind him, however, Hardy was still in Brest. His financial problems had been solved but the winds were unfavourable and he was unable to slip by the British blockade of the port. Humbert was now bereft of support and only the greatest good fortune could give him a chance of success.

CHAPTER 15

THE FRENCH AT LAST

22 August to 4 September 1798

General Humbert led his flotilla of three ships into Killala in north Mayo on 22 August and remained there at anchor through much of a calm and warm afternoon. Those who saw his ships sailing in, including the local Protestant bishop, Joseph Stock, did not realise for much of the day that they were French. After several hours the French soldiers started to come ashore and then the reason for their appearance became clearer. A handful of local yeomen offered token resistance but fled before a battle even developed. As soon as they got ashore in large numbers the French moved into the Castle, the strongest building in the town, and began to billet themselves in its lower floors and grounds. The Castle was the home of the bishop but he and his family were treated well.

Humbert announced to the townspeople that he had come to liberate them from the 'English yoke' and claimed to be acting in the name of 'France and the Blessed Virgin'. While this part of Mayo did have a skeletal United Irishmen organisation, the movement was not especially strong here and so the message of liberation was probably alien to many ears. The area did have an active group of Defenders, a result of the flight of Catholics from southern Ulster earlier in the decade but, given the poor organisational state of the Catholic Church in the region at this time, even the religious part of Humbert's message may have had less impact than he anticipated.

Humbert's first task was to get all of his equipment, which included several thousand stand of arms and ammunition, ashore. He tried unsuccessfully to force the bishop to order carts from the town and surrounding area to assemble at the shore. Next day, however, he requisitioned the carts and got everything transferred to land. Fortunately for him, even though the handful of local yeomanry had by now spread the word of his landing, government forces in the region were not well enough organised to attack him at this early stage.

Over the first twenty-four hours after the landing, hundreds of local United Irishmen and others, who were either Defenders anxious to join the cause or simply country people happy to get involved in what seemed to be an enticing

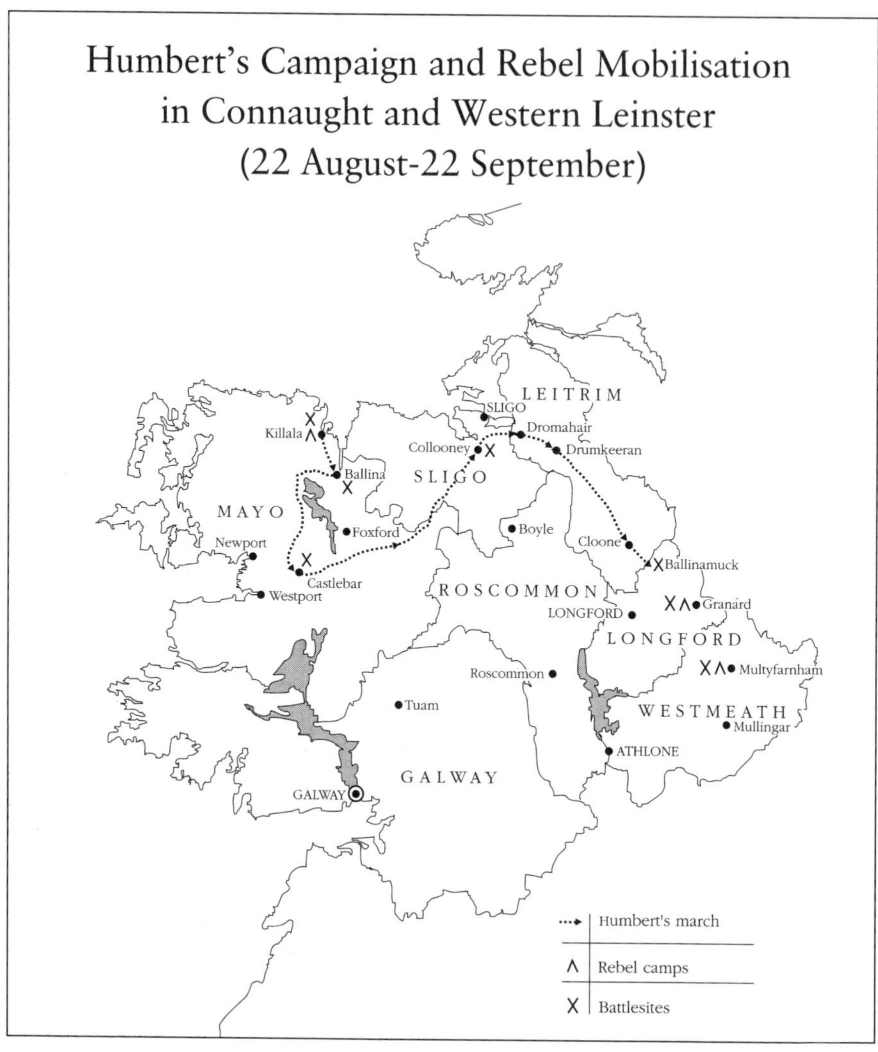

Humbert's Campaign and Rebel Mobilisation in Connaught and Western Leinster (22 August-22 September)

adventure, came to Humbert's headquarters and had arms and an assortment of uniforms distributed to them. At least some of these had enough faith in Humbert's assurances that his column was only the advance force for a much larger expedition (up to thirty thousand were mentioned as being on the way) that they threw aside any doubts about the chances of success and accepted what the French had to offer. For their part, the French took advantage of the country by requisitioning provisions for their men and horses with notes drawn on what they called the 'Provisional Government of Connaught', a body which, for the first two days or so after their landing, existed in their minds only.

The government's response to the landing was rapid and resolute. Cornwallis and Lake had learned of the French landing within twenty-four hours and responded by ordering militia and regular troop reinforcements out to Connaught immediately and to dispatch news of the landing and a request for even more British reinforcements to Pitt. They set out themselves for the West the next day, Friday, 24 August. Lake travelled by road, moving as quickly as he could with a small column of troops, while Cornwallis took the more leisurely route by the Grand Canal. In doing this they were demonstrating both how seriously they took the French threat (spies had reported a force of four thousand to be on the way to Ireland) and of how confident they were that the old rebellious counties along the east coast, even Wicklow where Holt and Dwyer still held out, would not present a new threat once their backs were turned. Initially, the commanders of the garrisons in northern Connaught, following the successful tactics of their counterparts in places like Wexford in the heyday of the rebellion, adopted a cautious approach. The garrison in Ballina, the nearest town to Killala, ten miles to the south, remained in place on 23 and 24 August, hesitant to move up to the French positions. The much larger garrison at Castlebar, a further twenty miles to the south, under the command of General Hutchinson, remained in place too, as did the garrison in Sligo, thirty miles to the east of Killala.

Saturday, 25 August 1798

On 25 August, as Lake and Moore were making their way westwards, Humbert and his officers with their United Irishmen allies suddenly went on the offensive. Humbert's instructions had been to avoid offensive action until Hardy had landed and made contact with him and he still assumed Hardy was on his way or had already landed. In these circumstances he might have stayed dug in at Killala until contact was made. However, his decision to break out of the little town was strategically sound as this would allow him to broaden the area of his control and to entice even more of the local population to join him. He marched due south, leading his eight hundred Frenchmen and several thousand Irish recruits straight at Ballina and leaving about two hundred men in Killala to guard his gunpowder supply. The Ballina garrison fled after putting up token resistance on a bridge to its north. They took their weapons with them but Humbert was now in possession of a beachhead ten miles deep and had an army of about six thousand men, many of them untrained and utterly inexperienced but, it also included his French veterans, who could be counted on not to break easily. There was still no sign of Hardy though and now, four days after the landing, this was becoming a concern, especially since Humbert learned that evening that government forces were converging on him from several points.

In fact, the government forces were not yet ready to go on the offensive. Lake was still a day's travel away from Co. Mayo and the garrisons in northern Connaught, including the substantial garrisons at Sligo to Humbert's east and

ERTY, EQUA[illegible], FRATERNITY, UNIO

IRISHMEN,

YOU have not forgot Bantry bay. You know what efforts France has made to afsist you.

Her affection for you, her desire of avenging your wrongs and assuring your independence can never be impaired.

After several unsuccessfull attempts, behold at last Frenchmen arrived amongst you.

They come to support your courage, to share your dangers, to join their arms and to mix their blood with yours in the sacred cause of liberty.

They are the forerunners of other Frenchmen, whom you shall soon enfold in your arms.

Brave IRISHMEN, our cause is common. Like you we abhor the avaricious and blood-thirsty policy of an oppressive governement. Like you we hold as indefeasible the right of all nations to liberty. Like you we are persuaded that the peace of the World shall ever be troubled as long as the British ministry is suffered to make with impunity a traffic of the industry, labour and blood of the people.

But exclusive of the same interests which unite us, we have powerfull motives to love and defend you.

Have we not been the pretext of the cruelty exercised against you by the Cabinet of St James? The heart-felt interest you have shown for the grand events of our revolution, has it not been imputed to you as a crime? Are not tortures and death continually hanging over such of you as are barely suspected of being our friends?

Let us unite then and march to glory.

We Swear [illegible] most inviolable re[illegible]ct for your properties, your laws and all yo[illegible] [illegible]igions opinions. Be free, be masters in your own country. We look for no other conquest than that of your Liberty, no other success tha[illegible]

The[illegible] [illegible]king your chains is arrived. Our triumphant troops are now flying [illegible] [illegible]mities of the earth to tear up the roots of the wealth and tyranny o[illegible] [illegible]es. That frightfull colossus is mouldering away in every part. Can [illegible] [illegible]y Irishman ba[illegible] [illegible]ough to seperate himself in such a happy conjunctu[illegible] [illegible] the grand in[illegible] of his country. If su[illegible] [illegible]ere be, brave friends, let him be chased from the [illegible]try he betrays and let his property become the reward of those generous men who know how to fight and die.

Irishmen, recollect the late defeats wich your ennemies have experienced from the French; recollect the plains of Honscoote, Toulon, Quiberon and Ostende; recollect America free from the moment she wished to be so. The contest between you and your oppressors cannot be long.

Union, Liberty, the Irish Republic. Such is our shout. Let us march. Our hearts are devoted to you; our glory is in your happiness.

Proclamation issued by Humbert on landing at Killala, Co Mayo.

Castlebar to his south, were very much on a defensive footing. In addition, news of the landing was continuing to spread and United Irishmen and those they were able to convince to join them were mobilising in numbers that might eventually offer a threat to the government forces.

Sunday, 26 August 1798

Convinced that he needed to strike at the chain of government posts around him rather than wait to be overwhelmed before Hardy arrived, Humbert decided to go on the offensive. On the afternoon of 26 August, he took a force of about fifteen hundred men, almost his entire French force and the pick of the Irish rebels, and moved out of Ballina to attack Castlebar, the largest town in Mayo, defended by a force of about seventeen hundred militia and yeomanry. Considering the fate of rebel attacks on well-defended towns in earlier phases of the rebellion, the odds were against Humbert at this point.

His approach to the problem was, however, unconventional and this may have compensated somewhat for his handicaps. Instead of driving due south along the main road from Killala and Ballina to Castlebar, he led his men along a series of mountain roads, many of them very poor, that took him around Lough Conn and allowed him to approach the town from the northwest, a direction from which the garrison did not anticipate his coming. The detour enabled him to bypass a sizeable garrison at Foxford Bridge, halfway between Castlebar and Ballina. He also counted on having the element of surprise on his side when he did attack.

Unaware that the town was about to be attacked, General Lake, after travelling frantically all day, reached Castlebar at about midnight while Cornwallis was still progressing slowly along the Grand Canal. The counties in the east, north and south of the country were remaining quiet, even though news of the French landing had now spread widely. The old rebels had evidently had too much of war and its consequences to attempt to bring such a scourge on their people again.

Monday, 27 August 1798

At dawn on Monday, Humbert and his fifteen hundred men suddenly appeared on a ridge to the northwest of Castlebar. News of his approach had reached the town a short while before and the garrison had time to wheel around to cover the defences in this direction. However, the defenders were not in a good position. Many of them were inexperienced militiamen and yeomen facing battle for the first time and were unnerved by Humbert's tactics and the fearsome reputation of the French soldiers which had preceded them.

Humbert threw his men at the defenders' lines at about eight o'clock.

Despite suffering early losses, the French troops intimidated the defenders to such an extent that some began to give ground and then, once they suffered the first casualties, to flee. Humbert's men, French and Irish alike, took advantage of the garrison's sudden collapse and swept into the town. The defenders suffered over fifty losses with several hundred men wounded or missing in the battle while most of the others fled along the road towards Tuam, leaving their weapons, artillery, ammunition and baggage behind them. Not since the Wexford rebels took Wexford town had a garrison of this size fled from the insurgents and in terms of the booty captured this was the most impressive rebel victory of the entire war.

For the rest of the day, Humbert had his men extend the trenches and other fortifications of the town. He had now driven thirty miles inland and had effectively taken the central half of Co. Mayo out of government control. In addition, the western third of the county, lying between Humbert's wedge and the Atlantic, was not garrisoned by the government and small units had mobilised there and were on the point of taking possession of Newport and Westport in the name of the rebels and their French allies. This was much more than Humbert had been instructed to attempt but since there was still no sign of Hardy and since the Irish population seemed to be responding to his flag Humbert might be forgiven for thinking that, with or without Hardy, he could yet inspire a native rebellion that would overthrow the government.

As for Hardy, he was still bottled up in Brest by the British fleet. Unknown to either him or Humbert, however, James Napper Tandy had already sailed from the French coast in a corvette carrying almost four hundred more French soldiers and a large supply of arms and ammunition. It was a small addition to whatever French force Tandy might find in the field when he got to Ireland but were the United Irishmen to rise on his appearance off the Irish coast, as Tandy boasted they would, his arrival would be certain to guarantee success for Humbert.

Tuesday, 28 August 1798

On Tuesday, as Tandy's ship ploughed its way westwards by the mouth of the Channel, Humbert remained on the defensive in Castlebar. Recruits kept joining his force as the grip of his Irish allies on the county tightened with each hour. Cornwallis, who had reached Tullamore the previous day and was now in Athlone, spent the day assessing the damage from the loss of Castlebar and planning a defensive strategy in the event of a further French advance. The government side now had sizeable garrisons at Tuam, Athlone, Boyle and Sligo and with reinforcements moving up from all parts of the country were in a good position to corner the French and their rebel allies.

James Napper Tandy: a leading Dublin radical in the 1780s and United Irishman in the 1790s. He became part of the delegation to France and sailed to the Donegal coast shortly after Humbert's landing in Mayo in a vain effort to revive the rebellion. When this failed, he left Ireland for good.

Wednesday, 29 August 1798

On 29 August, a week since the first French landing, Humbert held his ground for the second day in succession, keeping his own garrison at Castlebar behind their defences and maintaining the smaller garrisons at Ballina and Killala. Cornwallis spent the day making his way across Co. Galway to Tuam, where he arrived by evening. The government force there numbered about eight thousand men and, after being in retreat or on the defensive for three days, was getting prepared to go on the offensive itself.

Saturday, 1 September to Tuesday, 4 September 1798

Over the next four days, beginning on 1 September, a tense stand-off developed between the government forces and Humbert and his allies. Conscious of the need to wait for Hardy and anxious not to abandon his strong position, Humbert remained on the defensive. To reinforce his tie with the Irish rebels who made up the bulk of his forces, he created a Provisional Government of Connaught and appointed John Moore, the son of a prominent Catholic landlord, as its President. With Moore's cooperation, he now decreed military conscription for all men between sixteen and forty-five. Slowly but surely, in the absence of the main French force, Humbert was moving towards a more serious involvement with the Irish rebellion, of which he was now the chief architect.

On 4 September the stalemate was broken on several fronts. Cornwallis and Lake finally moved their eight thousand men out of the safety of Tuam and marched them about fifteen miles to the northwest in the direction of Castlebar, camping for the night about twelve miles from the town and preparing for an attack the next day. Humbert had plans of his own and when he realised the threat from Cornwallis he led his small but mobile and tough force north-eastwards from Castlebar towards Co. Sligo. He continued to scour the countryside for rebel support and even considered a dash out in the direction of Ulster to link up with the Presbyterians. Like the Wexford rebels a month earlier, he saw the people of Antrim and Down as his possible final salvation.

That very day in fact, the small United Irishmen organisation in Co. Longford and in parts of Co. Westmeath, places that had seen no serious movement earlier in the summer, began to mobilise. At first, only small units of a few hundred men in the vicinity of Edgeworthstown and in a few other centres joined up but it was the first such development outside Co. Mayo since the French landed and, with a large part of the government's forces now on the western side of the Shannon while Humbert was moving north-eastwards towards Sligo, it might have been a harbinger of serious problems to come for Lake and Cornwallis.

CHAPTER 16

THE LAST CHANCE

4 to 12 September 1798

The week from the fourth to the twelfth of September, with the harvest in full swing in much of the eastern part of the country, saw the last serious chance of success for the Irish rebellion disappear in a frantic series of marches and battles in the upper part of the Shannon valley. Fittingly, perhaps, the affair was as dramatic and as brutal at its end as it had been at its beginning.

Humbert and his force, made up of about eight hundred French soldiers and a thousand Irish rebels, marched across eastern Co. Mayo and southern Co. Sligo throughout the night of 4 and 5 September and maintained their rapid pace through all of the next day. They were stopped at Collooney, a few miles south of Sligo town, by a detachment of several hundred men from the local garrison. Humbert's soldiers overcame the government troops after a brief but intense battle in which the defenders had about fifty men killed and a hundred taken prisoner. However, almost as many of Humbert's men were killed and he had to free his prisoners in order to speed up his progress. As evening approached he pushed on eastwards and finally stopped at the village of Drumahair, just inside Co. Leitrim, and camped for the night. He and his men had marched over fifty miles since leaving Castlebar a day-and-a-half earlier.

Cornwallis had not been idle in the meantime. His plan was to take Castlebar on the fourth or fifth but as soon as he learned that Humbert was marching north-eastwards he split his force at Hollymount, giving Lake about half of them to pursue Humbert across Mayo and Sligo. He took the rest himself and marched due east to protect Dublin. This ensured that a sizeable government force would be close on Humbert's heels whether he was heading north or south. In the meantime, a small government detachment moved into Castlebar and took possession of the place virtually unopposed.

Meantime, the rebellion in Longford and Westmeath was rapidly gaining momentum. The Longford group, consisting of men from Longford itself and from neighbouring parts of Westmeath, had concentrated around Edgeworthstown but now shifted to a large camp near Granard, which held as

AN AUTHENTIC ACCOUNT

OF THE BEHAVIOUR, CONDUCT AND CONFESSION, OF

JAMES BEAGHAN,

Who was executed on Vinegar Hill,

ON SATURDAY THE 24th DAY OF AUGUST, 1799.

TAKEN BEFORE CHRISTIAN WILSON, ESQ. HIGH SHERIFF OF THE COUNTY OF WEXFORD,

AND J. H. LYSTER, ESQ. ONE OF THE JUSTICES OF THE PEACE FOR THE SAID COUNTY:

THE Day but one before his Execution, two Popish Priests went to visit him, and upon their entering his Cell, he exclaimed against them in these Words: "Begone ' from me you accursed, who have been the Cause of my Eternal Damnation, for ' were it not for you, I never would have been guilty of Murder."—Having so said, he turned from them, and requested that they might be put out, and in some short time after, he requested that Captain Boyd might be sent for, to whom he made the following Confession:

I JAMES BEAGHAN, acknowledge and confess that I am guilty of the Crime for which I am to suffer, but that I did not commit it from ill-will to the People that were murdered, but from the Order of * Luke Byrne; I could not disobey him—no Person dare refuse to obey the Orders of the Commanders. I am sure that any Man in Command could save the Lives of the Poor; every Man that was a Protestant was called an Orangeman, and every one was to be killed, from the poorest Man in the Country. Before the Rebellion, I never heard there was any hatred between Roman Catholics and Protestants, they always lived peaceably together. I always found the Protestants better Masters and more indulgent Land-lords than my own Religion; during the Rebellion, I never saw any one interfere to prevent Murder, but one Byrne who saved a Man. I think all that were present were as guilty as those that perpetrated the Murders. It was thinking that we were all equally guilty, that prevented me from flying the Country. The Women were numerous, and were as bad as the Men. The Rebels treated the Prisoners with great severity, very different from the way that I have been used in goal. They thought it no more a sin to kill a Protestant than a dog; had it not been that they were so soon quashed, they would have fought with each other for the Property of the Protestants. They were begining before the Battle of Vinegar Hill. Ever since the Rebellion, I never heard one of the Rebels express the least sorrow for what was done; on the contrary I have heard them say, they were sorry that whilst they had the Power they did not kill more, and that there were not half enough killed. I know that the Rebels were determined to rise if the French should come; and I believe they did not give up half their arms. There are Guns, Bayonets and Pikes hid in the Country.

*** Now Gentlemen, remember what I tell you, if you and the Protestants are ever in the Power of the Catholics again, as they are now in yours, they will not leave one of you alive; you will all go smack smooth, even them that campaigned with them, if things had gone well with them, would in the end have been killed. I have heard them say so many times.

Taken before us, Aug. 23, 1799.
CHRISTIAN WILSON, Sheriff.
J. H. LYSTER, Justice P.

his
JAMES ✗ BEAGHAN
mark.

(A Copy.)

Having arrived at the place of Execution, Captain Boyd brought him aside, and read his Confession, and asked him if it was correctly taken down, to which he answered in the affirmative. Just as the Executioner was about to turn him off, he called out saying, "stop," and lifting up his Cap, said with a very loud Voice, "Captain Boyd, " you have taken down my Confession perfectly correct; if it was not for the Priests I " never would have been guilty of Murder, nor have dragged five unfortunate Persons out of the Windmill to be murdered; amongst these five, were the Son of Old Minchin the Carpenter.

* Luke Byrne a Commander in the Rebels.

*** From this Mark Beaghan spoke without having been asked any questions, and spoke with an earnestness and in a manner that shewed his sincerity.

Price Two-pence

Beaghan's 'Account': although Beaghan may well have committed atrocities, the tone of this document may primarily reflect the atmosphere of the 'White Terror' which reigned after the Rebellion.

Bartle (Bartholomew) Teeling: son of a prominent Catholic merchant from Belfast and an early member of the United Irishmen and part of the delegation in France. He landed with Humbert and, captured following the Battle of Ballinamuck, he was hanged.

many as six thousand men by evening. They were not well organised and not well armed but they were as large a force as the United Irishmen and their Defender allies had been able to put into the field anywhere in the opening stages of the rebellion. Simultaneously, a rebel force of about the same size had gathered on the demesne of Wilson's Hospital, outside Mullingar in Co. Westmeath.

The mobilisation caused great confusion among the government commanders in the area. They were well aware of the danger from Mayo and realised how large the local rebel forces had grown but most of them were indecisive. The Mullingar garrison that might have taken the initiative immediately remained in the town and made no effort to deal with the growing rebel force at Wilson's Hospital. Two small government columns did eventually move out to confront the rebels. A detachment of about a hundred yeomen moved south towards Mullingar from Castlepollard, about ten miles to the north, and a larger detachment, consisting of about three hundred and fifty Highlanders and yeomen, moved down from Cavan town, about twenty-five miles to the north. While these might weaken the government's efforts to contain Humbert now that he was on the move, they also made it less likely that he could link up with the Longford and Westmeath rebel armies when he learned of their whereabouts.

On 6 September Humbert marched his force from Drumahair to Drumkeeran, still inside Co. Leitrim but now clearly moving in a south-easterly direction. He had learned that the rebellion in Longford and Westmeath was serious and was diverting from the route to Ulster to try to link up with it. Cornwallis was moving eastwards, too, although he was still on the west side of the Shannon at this point. So, too, was Lake who continued to tail Humbert but avoided a pitched battle.

With their numbers still mounting, the leaders of the Longford rebels now decided to launch an attack on the garrison of about two hundred and fifty men in Granard. They were even more poorly armed than their comrades at Arklow and New Ross two months earlier and they could make no headway against the well-equipped soldiers. Panic eventually broke out in their ranks and they began to flee. The mounted yeomen from the garrison and even the infantry then came out and cut them down by the hundreds as they tried to get away in the confusion. Around four hundred men were massacred by the garrison before the day was over. As at Carlow at the outbreak of the war, the repulse was so total and so destructive that the Longford rebel movement totally collapsed. However, the other rebel army of about six thousand men was still intact outside Mullingar and with them and his own forces there was still a possibility that Humbert might threaten the government.

The chance of such a victory began to erode rapidly. Next day Humbert and his men conducted another dramatic march, leaving Drumkeeran early in the morning, crossing the Shannon at Ballintra around the middle of the day and finally stopping for the night at Cloon, about ten miles northwest of Granard and about thirty miles from Mullingar. Cornwallis got across the Shannon during the day too, although a little later than Humbert, and Lake kept up his cautious pursuit of the French general.

Fortunately for the government side, the rebel force in Mullingar had been already as thoroughly destroyed as their comrades at Granard the day before. Government detachments from Castlepollard and Cavan converged on them during the day and the rebels deserted by the thousands even before the soldiers got within range. A remnant held their ground on the demesne but the soldiers had them badly outgunned and the battle quickly turned into a massacre, at least two hundred of the rebel force being killed. By evening Humbert was utterly cut off in his camp at Cloon. He had small garrisons still in place at Ballina and Killala but these were at least three days' march behind him and he had a force of about ten thousand government troops, ranged to his north, south and east, to contend with. With no word of Hardy from any direction, he realised the cause was now lost.

Humbert's part in the war came to a close the next morning at a place called

Ballinamuck, about halfway between Cloon and Granard, when he drew his army up on a low hill to fight a token resistance against the approaching government forces. The battle was brief, no longer than half an hour, and government and French casualties were light. The thousand or so Irish rebels suffered the brunt of the fighting and once again hundreds of them were set upon by the well-armed soldiers and slaughtered without mercy in the final phases of the battle. The French, in contrast, surrendered formally and were offered the dignities of prisoners of war. Humbert's Irish adventure was at an end but he could look back his efforts with satisfaction, especially considering that Hardy's Brest expedition had not materialised. For the rebels and the country people associated with the rising, however, there followed the usual campaign of counter-revolution, complete with the summary executions, house burnings and general terrorising that had been conducted in every area where rebellion had taken place to date.

Over the next several days, Cornwallis and Lake assessed their situation from the vantage point of the midlands. No rebel movement of any significance had developed anywhere outside northern Connaught and northwest Leinster. All of Ulster, the rest of Leinster, all of Munster and the southern part of Connaught had remained tranquil. Humbert and his eight hundred men spent these days being transported by canal barge to Dublin, whence they would be shipped back to France. There was still the possibility of an imminent second French landing to consider while some two hundred of Humbert's men and their rebel allies retained a foothold in northern Mayo but, otherwise, the government once again seemed to be in a strong position. Cornwallis and Lake decided to move back to the capital themselves and left John Moore in command of a sizeable force at Moate in Co. Westmeath to keep a watchful eye on the immediate area. The Viceroy also sent a small force westwards, under a Colonel Trench, to deal with the rebel footholds at Ballina and Killala. Over the next few days Trench made his way cautiously towards Castlebar, as Moore remained in the midlands and as Cornwallis, Lake and the captured French moved slowly towards Dublin.

Over the next two weeks there was an air of epilogue to the war. The French garrison remained in place at Killala and the large rebel camp continued to attract recruits. Apart from their outpost at Ballina, ten miles to the south, though, and some small rebel detachments in the mountains on either side of the broad valley between the two towns, this ten-mile-long corridor was all the territory the rebels would hold onto over the two weeks after Ballinamuck. This enclave would have not withstood an attack for long but the government forces were still concerned with the likelihood of a new and much larger French landing so the task of dealing with Ballina and Killala would have to wait.

There was no significant fighting over the first three days after the battle of Ballinamuck but on 12 September a sizeable rebel force launched a sudden attack on the small garrison in Castlebar. They were unable to dislodge the soldiers, however, and eventually pulled back after losing several dozen men. The following three days saw no new developments: the strong rebel force, several thousand strong, as well as the small French force now hopelessly trapped in Killala waited for news of French ships approaching from the Atlantic.

On 16 September, unknown to either the French or the rebels at Killala, the long-awaited expedition from Brest finally departed. It had fewer troops on board than originally planned, less than three thousand, and Hardy had been replaced as commander by General Bompard. However, after years of frustration, Wolfe Tone was finally making his way back to Ireland as part of an invasion force. But the departure was already a month behind schedule and the fleet was at least a week or two sailing time from the Irish coast.

The next afternoon, however, Napper Tandy's corvette, with its three hundred French troops and supply of arms and ammunition, sailed into Rutland Bay in Co. Donegal, completing the journey from Dunkirk in twelve days. There was no garrison in the little village of Rutland and Tandy landed without incident. That night he heard conflicting stories about what had happened to Humbert but next day learned that the French had been defeated and surrendered. Even so, scores of people from the immediate locality expressed enthusiasm for renewing the struggle but Tandy and the French officers with him decided that the chances of success were now too slim. That afternoon they boarded their ship again and sailed away, making their way around the northern coast of Ireland and Scotland and returning to France by way of the North Sea.

For the next five days, as Bompard and Tone ploughed through the September seas and covered the first fifth or so of their voyage to Ireland, government forces in Mayo got ready to eliminate the last remaining rebel positions at Ballina and Killala. They were still cautious but Trench made his move from Castlebar on 22 September, exactly a month since Humbert's landing, sweeping into Ballina the next morning and taking the town with ease. From there he pushed northwards to Killala in driving rain but he reached the edge of the town that afternoon and launched the last attack of the last battle of the 1798 Rebellion, indeed the last significant pitched battle in Irish history.

A large part of the rebel force melted away at the news of the army's approach and by the time Trench opened his assault his twelve hundred men had a clear numerical advantage over the eight hundred or so remaining rebels, since the two hundred French and their officers took little or no part in the struggle. As the soldiers advanced steadily, the rebels were unable to use their pikes and their badly aimed shots did little damage. Finding themselves in an untenable position, they began to retreat and then to flee. The 'battle', if it can be so called, soon developed in a familiar and tragic pattern. Yet again, broken and fleeing, helpless

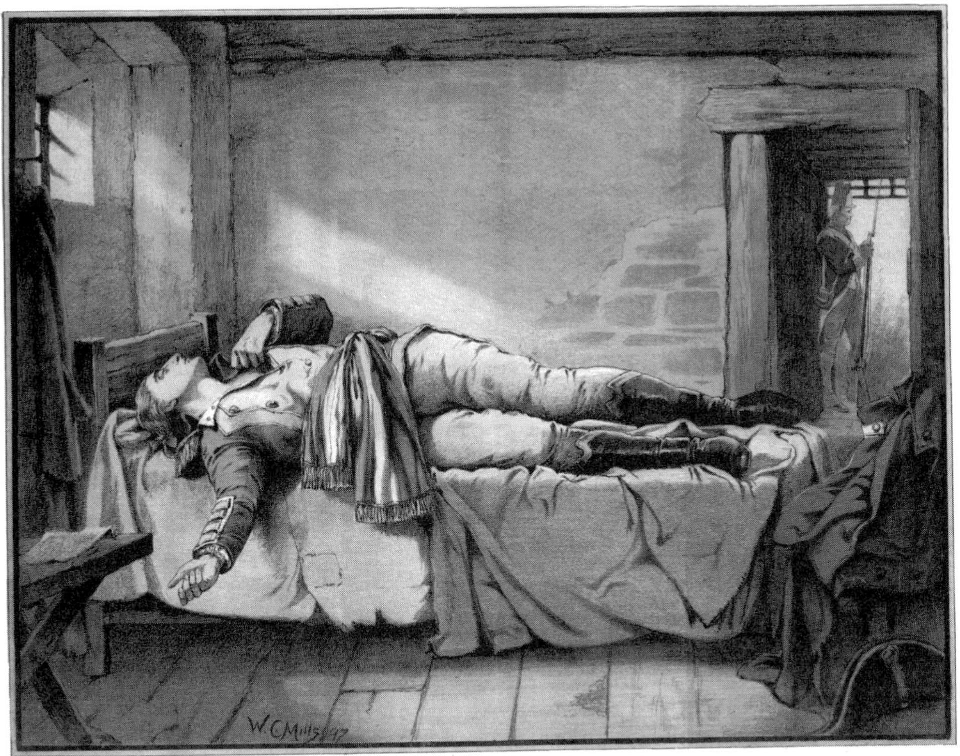

Death of Wolfe Tone: here nationalists of the 1890s have elevated him to a Washington-like heroic status.

rebels were cut down by sword and musket as they tried to escape or attempted to surrender. Men died by the score in the streets of the little town and scores more died in the surrounding fields or along the shoreline. When it was finally over between four and six hundred of them had fallen. The government side lost only a handful.

Over the next several days, the soldiers searched the hamlets and isolated cabins in the region around Killala and hunted down and killed even more rebels or men suspected of having been rebels. Scores of men and women not involved in the fighting fell victim too and the usual spate of executions took place. John Moore, the erstwhile President of Connaught, was among those hanged after a hurried trial. A popular young rebel commander named Ferdy O'Dowd was shot in a field near the town. In a few days the amnesty policy was applied and ordinary rebels crept back to their cabins to rebuild their lives. However, the last battle had been fought and the last massacre of fleeing men had taken place.

There would be a post-script. Bompard, Tone and their little fleet battled the early autumn seas and the British navy for four weeks after their departure from Brest and finally made their way into Lough Swilly, off the coast of Donegal, on 12 October. There they were attacked by a British flotilla that defeated them after a ten-hour battle. The entire French force, including Wolfe Tone, was captured. A month later, on 8 November, Tone was brought to Dublin and tried for treason. He was condemned to death on 10 November but cut his own throat in his cell two days later. His wound was not immediately fatal and he lingered in agony for a week, finally dying on 19 November.

By the time of Tone's death the chances of another and more serious French expedition being launched against the Irish government, or indeed any part of the British Isles, was gone. News of the dramatic annihilation of the French fleet at the mouth of the Nile had reached England early in October. This British victory meant that the seaborne threat to England was at an end; it also ensured that French dominance in Europe was about to be challenged not only by Britain but by other powers, such as Austria and Prussia, that had remained quiescent now for over a year. Whatever was to happen in Ireland would almost certainly happen without the French entering into the game. The dramatic phase in the history of the British Isles that had opened with the Bantry Bay expedition in late 1796 had finally drawn to a close.

CHAPTER 17

LEGACIES: 1798-1998

The death of Wolfe Tone brought the United Irish movement to an end but the war which the movement had launched had a long afterglow. For several years, rebel bands of various sizes held out in the mountain and wooded fastnesses of Wicklow, Wexford and Carlow. The Wicklow hold-outs under Michael Dwyer were subdued only in 1803 when Dwyer was transported to New South Wales and a Wexford band led by an old rebel named Corcoran was not hunted down until 1804. The abortive rebellion organised by Robert Emmet, the younger brother of Thomas Addis Emmet, in Dublin in 1803 was an effort to rekindle the movement but it never spread beyond a small area of the city and it became best known for the speech from the dock of its condemned leader.

The government's campaign of repression and the local campaigns of ultra-loyalists lasted for years too. Occasional executions of former rebels, usually on atrocity charges, took place in 1799 and in the early years of the new century whilst the more militant bands of yeomanry kept up an intense anti-rebel campaign in counties like Wicklow and Wexford for a long time. The Wexford loyalists continued to celebrate the anniversary of the major battles of the rebellion there into the second decade of the nineteenth century.

The generation that had fought in the summer of 1798 lived the rest of their lives in its shadow. Many of them had been in their twenties and thirties during the decade of revolution so most of them reached middle-age around the time of Waterloo and were old men by the 1820s and 1830s. Only the longest-lived saw the 1840s and 1850s.

Those who did live longest, though, survived to see great changes, some of which brought about things they had fought for; other developments would have been bitterly disappointing. Perhaps the most important immediate result of the Rising was the passage in 1800 of the Act of Union, which merged the Irish and British parliaments and which was a massive setback for the separatists among the former rebels. The Union was accompanied by a vague promise to the Catholic hierarchy and the wealthier members of the community that they would soon be granted the right to take seats in parliament. Whether this would have been of much real comfort to men whose movement had been opposed by those same Catholics is unclear but the fact that this promise had still not been realised when King George III died in 1820 must have been very disillusioning.

However, the campaign for Catholics to have the right to enter parliament, launched by Daniel O'Connell in the 1820s, would have inspired many of the old rebels, especially those who had a close connection with the Defender movement. Several old rebel officers, among them Thomas Cloney of Wexford, became heavily involved in O'Connell's organisation. On the other hand, those who supported the non-sectarian convictions of the United Irishmen movement would regard the mobilisation of the Catholic population by a skilful politician like O'Connell as disconcerting, especially since by this time the Presbyterians of Ulster were going their own way.

The political reorientation of the Presbyterians in the new century is perhaps the most surprising change of all. In the 1790s they were more dedicated to republicanism and revolution than either the Catholic or Protestant populations. By the 1820s and 1830s this enthusiasm had waned and by the 1840s the children and grandchildren of the Presbyterian rebel generation had come to identify more closely with their Protestant lineage and had come to regard the union with Britain as wholly beneficial. This may partly account for both the delay in the granting of Catholic emancipation and for the subsequent politicisation and mobilisation of the 'Catholic nation', both for emancipation in the 1820s and the repeal of the Union in the 1840s. It may also explain the rapid economic development which eastern Ulster experienced, particularly since the welfare of the region became so obviously tied to the great marketplace of the British Empire. The generation of Presbyterians that grew to maturity in the 1820s and 1830s would also have had a rather different view of the French and American republican traditions. The excesses of the Jacobins had become a serious liability by this time and religious dissenters tended to become constitutional monarchists rather than outright republicans. In addition, Presbyterian emigration ended after the 1790s so that the sentimental attachment between the Presbyterian communities in Ireland and America waned. The end result was that former rebels, Presbyterian, Catholic or Anglican, who lived until the 1840s and who had fought for a nation in which all religions were to be equally tolerated, survived to witness an Ireland in which the divide between Catholic and Protestant began to yawn very wide indeed.

The rebels who lived to see the 1840s also suffered the agony of witnessing the social and economic catastrophe of the Great Famine and its consequences. William Farrell, a former Co. Carlow rebel and the author of one of the most poignant memoirs of the rebellion, noted in the 1830s that the tradesmen of the Irish countryside were already losing their livelihood at that point and that there was a remarkable decline in living standards in his region. The same was happening in every area where the rebellion had broken out with the exception of eastern Ulster.

It is difficult to surmise how the rebel generation looked back on 1798 as they aged. Without question, there was great pride in what they had achieved on the battlefield and early on there emerged the sort of 'lost cause' mystique common in the wake of such conflicts. This pride is evident in the memoirs of Miles Byrne, the eighteen-year-old rebel in 1798. Writing in the Paris of the Second Empire, he stressed the military achievements of the rebels and hinted that the loss of the war was due, more than anything else, to the foolish mistakes of the leaders. William Farrell also blamed them but for deluding the countrypeople into fighting for a hopeless cause. His comments suggest that, in spite of the pride they may have felt at their achievements, many an old rebel may have lived to regret the destruction the rebellion actually brought about.

In spite of this, 1798 became sacred to Irish nationalists, whether parliamentary or revolutionary, of the mid to late nineteenth century, the grandchildren and great-grandchildren of the rebel generation. They lionised all the prominent rebel leaders and in 1898, the centenary of the rebellion, engaged in a fever of monument-building and commemorative marches that revived the memory of '98 and gave it a place of honour it may not have had previously. Catholic clergy became very much involved in the commemoration, an ironic twist given the attitude of the original United Irishmen to sectarianism and of the Catholic Church to them.

The independence movement of 1916-1922, although different in its approach and its values from the United Irishmen movement, ensured that 1798 would remain sacred in the Ireland of the twentieth century and it is not surprising that there were major celebrations of anniversaries of the rising in Co. Wexford in 1938 and 1948. What was perhaps being lost in these celebrations, however, was a sense that the 1798 Rising was a pan-Irish movement and that Anglicans and Presbyterians had as much right as Catholics to commemorate it. In addition, a tendency has developed to treat the 1798 Rising as primarily a Wexford rebellion, neglecting the struggles in many other counties. Lacking too, perhaps, has been the recognition that 1798 was part of a much wider American and European revolutionary movement designed to bring about a world in which people were free to choose their rulers and to enjoy the fruits of their labours.

The ideas of the 1790s are now accepted throughout the Western world. The great transformation from a world ruled by a privileged few to a world ruled by 'the people' has come very slowly, however. After the collapse of the French Revolution with the fall of Bonaparte in 1814, for about sixty years the old elites held onto power. The United States led the way to change in the 1820s by

Monument to William McNevin in New York: he was one of several former United Irishmen who went into exile after the Rising.

decreeing that a man could vote regardless of whether he had property or not. In Britain and Ireland the election laws were altered in 1829 to allow Catholics to sit in parliament and upper middle-class townspeople were given the vote in 1832. The Chartist campaign to give votes to all males became a powerful force in English life between 1836 and 1848 but faltered in the end. Revolutions in France in 1830 and 1848 extended voting rights, though universal male suffrage came to Western Europe only in the 1870s and 1880s. A democracy that included women would finally come only in the 1920s and democracy in a real sense began to emerge in eastern Europe only after 1989, exactly two hundred years after the French Revolution.

The United Irishmen believed in separatism and republicanism as well as in democracy and it is more difficult to determine where the world stands today in terms of these values. In spite of a few quaint but impressive survivals, monarchy has faded from almost the entire globe and its few survivals are swamped in a sea of republicanism of various kinds. Separatism, which has evolved into nationalism, has undergone many convolutions, from the simplistic romantic nationalism that emerged around the time of the French Revolution to the more ominous kinds of nationalism which developed in much of Europe in the late nineteenth and twentieth centuries. This kind of nationalism would have been anathema to the true United Irishmen, whose separatism was based on the notion of liberty in a universal sense and maintained that each people should be free to determine its own destiny.

The United Irishmen's sense of national freedom may have more relevance to our time than we are inclined to think. The notion of sisterhood among neighbouring republics is surely central to the modern 'European idea'. Based on a common set of principles concerning the rights of the citizen and the worker, this 'idea' assumes that the peoples of Europe, in spite of their many differences, can some day come to live with each other peacefully and work together towards common prosperity, all the while respecting each other's territory and national rights. This may be the only realistic solution to what some still call the 'Irish Question'. It is simplistic to argue that the principles of the United Irishmen are the principles of any particular group or organisation in either part of Ireland today. It is not at all unrealistic, however, to conclude that the solutions which must be found to the problems of both parts of Ireland must embrace the principles of tolerance, democracy and the peaceful coexistence of free peoples, principles that emerged out of the Enlightenment and that have come to be so broadly accepted in the late twentieth century. If that were to be accepted throughout the island of Ireland, the sacrifices of the men of '98 would not have been in vain.

1798: CHRONOLOGY OF EVENTS

Monday, 12 March Raid on Oliver Bond's and arrest of most of the Leinster Directory.

Friday, 30 March Country declared to be in a 'state of rebellion'.

Monday, 23 April Abercromby replaced as commander-in-chief of government forces by General Lake.

Thursday, 17 May United Irishmen make a decision to rebel on 23 May.

Saturday, 19 May Lord Edward Fitzgerald arrested.

Sunday, 20 May Sheares brothers arrested.

Wednesday, 23 May Final plans for Rising. Abortive attempt at Rising in Dublin: mail coaches stopped at Santry and Naas. Early stages of rebel mobilisation in Kildare, Wicklow and Meath.

Thursday, 24 May Rebels take possession of the Dunboyne/Dunshaughlin area of Meath, all of Co. Kildare (except towns of Naas, Athy and Monasterevin) and parts of northern and western Wicklow. News of rebellion spreads to outlying counties; rebels mobilise in southern Kildare and Wicklow and southern Carlow by nightfall. Government commander shoots two dozen soldiers (rebel suspects) at Dunlavin, Co. Wicklow.

Friday, 25 May Rebel attacks on Carlow town, Hacketstown, Monasterevin and Portarlington fail. Midlands rebels form large camps at Tara (Co. Meath), Timahoe, Gibbet Rath and Knockallen (Co. Kildare) and Blackmoor Hill (Co. Wicklow). Government troops massacre prisoners at Carnew; news of mobilisation reaches Co. Wexford.

Saturday, 26 May Camden in Dublin and rebel forces around city maintain positions and avoid offensive action. Early stages of rebel mobilisation take place in central Wexford. Rest of country remains quiet. Rebel camp at Tara attacked at twilight and scattered by Highland troops.

Sunday (Whit), 27 May Rebels in midlands lose control of Rathangan, Blessington and Ballitore – Knockallen rebels send word to General Dundas of their wish to surrender. Wexford rebels mass at Kilthomas and are defeated in the morning but a large camp at Oulart repels and annihilates government force.

Monday, 28 May Government forces and rebels in Kildare engage in stand-off; Walpole sent out from Dublin to stiffen Dundas's resolve; Duff sets out from Limerick to attack rebels from West. Wexford rebels consolidate at Scarawalsh and overwhelm Enniscorthy.

Tuesday, 29 May Knockallen rebels in Kildare surrender peacefully to Dundas; Wexford rebels camp at Vinegar Hill but march to Forth Mountain and threaten Wexford town by evening. Ulster United Irishmen meet at Armagh and decide to prepare for a Rising.

Wednesday, 30 May Wexford rebels capture Wexford town and garrison escapes to Duncannon Fort. Dundas accepts surrender of rebels at Gibbet Rath but Duff arrives and massacre of unarmed insurgents ensues.

Thursday, 31 May Wexford rebels appoint Bagenal Harvey as commander-in-chief and send divisions to Carrigrew Hill and Taghmon. Midlands rebellion fizzling out. Preparations still ongoing in Ulster; rest of country quiet.

Friday, 1 June Southern division of Wexford rebels marches to Carrickbyrne; northern division repulsed at Newtownbarry and Ballyminaun. Lake sets in motion three-pronged attack on Wexford rebels (i.e. Loftus, Walpole, Ancram). Antrim United Irishmen meet at Parkgate but still not ready to rise.

Saturday, 2 June Wexford rebels remain in camp. Antrim United leaders gather and are harangued by a mob of impatient followers at Ballyeaston. McCracken takes over Antrim movement and prepares to rise. Lake orders Johnson to move from Waterford to New Ross and Loftus, Walpole and Ancram converge on northern Wexford.

Sunday, 3 June Wexford rebels stay in camp at Carrickbyrne and Carrigrew. Lord Kingsborough captured in Wexford Harbour; situation in country at large clearer now to rebel leaders. Ulster rebels still quietly preparing to rise. Government forces in place to attack Wexford rebels by evening: Loftus and Walpole at Gorey, Ancram at Newtownbarry, Johnson at New Ross.

Monday, 4 June Carrigrew rebels smash government attack on northern Wexford at Battle of Tubberneering: Walpole killed; Loftus evacuates to Tullow; rebels form camp at Gorey; government forces abandon Arklow. Carrickbyrne rebels march to New Ross during evening.

Tuesday, 5 June Southern division of Wexford rebels attacks New Ross and is beaten back with great losses; rebel guarding party massacres loyalist prisoners at Scullabogue, six miles away. Northern Wexford rebels remain in Gorey camp. Ulster rebels still preparing to rise; Dickson, rebel leader in Down, arrested. Needham marches from Loughlinstown to Wicklow Town.

Wednesday, 6 June Final preparations for Rising taking place in Antrim; government commanders become aware of details. Wexford rebels stay in camps. Needham and his thousand-man column reach and fortify Arklow. Lord Edward Fitzgerald dies in prison.

Thursday, 7 June McCracken's Antrim rebels mobilise and take Larne, Randalstown and Ballymena; large rebel camp formed at Donegore Hill by afternoon but attack on Antrim town, launched from here, collapses; rebel mobilisation in eastern Co. Derry but quickly collapses. Southern Wexford rebels stay in camp; northern division attacks and burns Carnew; Bagenal Harvey replaced as commander-in-chief by Edward Roche.

Friday, 8 June Antrim rebellion unravels and Down United Irishmen, unaware of this, prepare to rise under Munro the following day. Northern division of Wexford rebels returns to Gorey from Carnew; southern division moves from Carrickbyrne to Slieve Coilte. Government forces in Belfast, Arklow, Newtownbarry and New Ross maintain cautious stance.

Saturday, 9 June Northern division of Wexford rebels attacks Arklow, driven back with heavy losses. Co. Down rebellion begins with rebel capture of Saintfield and Newtownards and failed attack on Portaferry. Rebel units mobilise in small detachments in southern Down. Napoleon reaches Malta.

Sunday, 10 June Down rebels take Bangor and camp at Saintfield grows to seven thousand men. Northern division of Wexford rebels remains encamped at Gorey; southern division remains at Slieve Coilte. Government gunboats bombard Fethard.

Monday, 11 June Down rebels consolidate grip on north-eastern part of Wexford and move camp to Ballynahinch. Northern division of Wexford rebels remains at Gorey; southern division moves from Slieve Coilte to Lacken Hill, near New Ross. Government forces at Belfast, Arklow, New Ross, etc. remain in defensive posture.

Tuesday, 12 June General Nugent suddenly goes on offensive in Down and surrounds rebels at Ballynahinch. Southern division of Wexford rebels sends raiding party to Borris, Co. Carlow but fails to acquire arms; northern division moves from Gorey to Limerick Hill. Government commanders at Arklow, Tullow, Newtownbarry and New Ross maintain defensive posture.

Wednesday, 13 June Nugent attacks and overwhelms rebel force at Ballynahinch; hundreds killed; Down rebellion unravels. Both Wexford rebel divisions remain in camp. Government forces around Wexford maintain defensive posture.

Thursday, 14 June Down rebellion peters out. Wexford rebels remain in camp. Rebel leaders in Wexford Town respond positively to a government emissary but emerging militant faction under Thomas Dixon sabotages contact.

Friday, 15 June Rebels remain in main camps in Wexford; small detachment from Limerick Hill force moves to Mountpleasant, near Tinahely, Co. Wicklow. Rift widens between moderate faction in Wexford town, under Matthew Keogh, and militant group under Dixon.

Saturday, 16 June Some violence breaks out between moderate and militant rebels in Wexford town. Southern division of Wexford rebels remains at Lacken Hill for fifth day. Northern division marches from Limerick Hill to Mountpleasant. In evening, first of British reinforcements arrives in Dublin Bay; General Lake prepares to move against Wexford as a result.

Sunday, 17 June Mountpleasant division of Wexford rebels captures and burns Tinahely; moderates gain upper hand in struggle with militants in Wexford town. Lake initiates move against Wexford rebels: joins Dundas at Blessington and marches to Hacketstown, Duff moves towards Newtownbarry, John Moore marches to Waterford.

Monday, 18 June Moore reaches New Ross; Loftus, Dundas and Lake reach Carnew; Duff reaches Newtownbarry; Needham maintains position at Arklow. Rebels at Tinahely remove to Kilcavan Hill, near Carnew. Rebel leadership decides on last stand at Vinegar Hill and instructs Kilcavan force to retreat.

Tuesday, 19 June Rain falls for first time in weeks. Government offensive begins with stunning success: Needham captures Gorey, Loftus moves as far as Carnew, Moore sweeps rebels from Lacken Hill and Carrickbyrne and camps at Foulkesmills, all without resistance. Northern rebels retreat as far as Camolin; southern division flees all the way from Lacken to Wexford town.

Wednesday, 20 June Lake moves Needham to Oulart and gathers Duff, Loftus and Dundas at Scarawalsh; Johnson moves from New Ross to western outskirts of Enniscorthy; northern rebels retreat to Vinegar Hill and avoid open battle; southern rebels rally and meet Moore at Goff's Bridge and eventually lose hard-fought battle. Dixon and followers massacre over ninety loyalists on Wexford bridge while battle taking place.

Thursday, 21 June Needham joins Lake for attack on Vinegar Hill; rebels defeated and retreat to Wexford town. Moore reaches outskirts of Wexford town by evening. Rebels flee in two columns: one towards south, a second northwards along coast. Some rebel leaders abandon cause.

Friday, 22 June Lake enters Wexford town; first executions of former rebels. Rebel columns slip away to Scullogue Gap (on Carlow border) and Croghan Mountain (on Wicklow border). Atrocities committed by both sides in northern Wexford. Cornwallis replaces Camden as viceroy.

Saturday, 23 June Rebel columns march from Scullogue Gap to Ridge of Leinster (near Castlecomer) and from Croghan to Ballymanus (in southern Wicklow). Executions continue in Wexford town.

Sunday, 24 June Rebel column attacks Castlecomer and takes town but with many losses and for little gain; second column marches to point near Hacketstown in preparation for attack. Lake continues arrests and trials of former rebel officers; Harvey captured on Saltee Islands.

Monday, 25 June Nine leading rebel officers hanged in Wexford town. Castlecomer rebel column retreats as far as Kilcumney Hill, in southern Carlow. Column in southern Wicklow attacks and fails to take Hacketstown.

Tuesday, 26 June Rebel column in southern Carlow routed in surprise attack and hundreds of non-combatants massacred by troops. Rebel column in southern Wicklow camps at Croghan for second time. More trials of former rebel officers in Wexford town.

Wednesday, 27 June Grogan and Harvey trials completed; both sentenced to hang next day. Rebels at Croghan remain in camp. Lake leaves Wexford town for Dublin; General Hunter takes command of trials and mop-up operation.

Thursday, 28 June Leading rebels (Grogan, Harvey, Colclough) executed in Wexford town. Hunter sends detachments to garrison northern Wexford towns.

Friday, 29 June Redeployments of government forces in northern Wexford completed.

Saturday, 30 June Needham (at Gorey) has rebel camp at Croghan reconnoitred before dawn; decides to attack. Rebels move after sunrise and surprise and overwhelm a cavalry unit pursuing them at Ballyellis. Rebels camp for night on Kilcavan Hill.

Sunday, 1 July Rebels remain at Kilcavan. Government forces stay in camps.

Monday, 2 July Rebels march across Shillelagh barony and defeat yeomanry force at Ballyraheen; fail to storm Chamney's house, near Shillelagh village; return to Croghan camp by nightfall.

Tuesday, 3 July Remnant of Kilcumney column reaches Croghan; two officers (Fitzgerald and Garret Byrne) leave at nightfall for Killoughram. Government forces remain in camps.

Wednesday, 4 July Rebels await return of Byrne and Fitzgerald at Croghan; small detachment burns gold-rush huts on northern slope.

Thursday, 5 July Byrne, Fitzgerald and Fr Mogue Kearns return before dawn. Needham prepares to attach rebel camp after dawn. Rebels move out towards Wicklow Gap at first light; stopped by Duff and fight indecisive Battle of Ballygullen. Final rebel gathering on Carrigrew results. Last units slip into Wicklow close to midnight.

Friday, 6 July Main rebel column marches deep into Wicklow; straggler units move towards glens. Government forces stay on defensive.

Saturday/Sunday, 7/8 July Government forces still on defensive, on Lake's orders. Rebels make way to Borleas, near Blessington, and join with Wicklow and Kildare units.

Monday, 9 July Lake moves south to Ferns to coordinate campaign, orders Moore to leave Taghmon and Needham to move to Rathdrum; Moore reaches Enniscorthy. Rebels leave Blessington and camp for night in central Kildare.

Tuesday, 10 July Rebels reach Timahoe Bog and join Kildare rebels under William Aylmer. Lake and Moore meet at Ferns and march to Carnew.

Wednesday, 11 July Rebels attach Clonard, Co. Meath, and are repulsed with heavy losses; camp by evening on Carbury Hill; many Wicklowmen leave for mountains. Lake and Moore pass through Hacketstown and camp at western approach to glens by nightfall.

Thursday, 12 July Rebels march via Rynville to Dunboyne, Co. Meath and stop for night. Lake and Moore scour Glenmalure but find no rebels.

Friday, 13 July Rebels march across Meath and camp for night on Meath/Louth border; pursued now by government forces.

Saturday, 14 July, Rebels resume march to Ulster but trapped at Knightstown, Co. Louth, and scattered; small detachment retreats south but defeated and scattered at Ballyboghill, Co. Dublin.

15 July–21 August Executions of rebel leaders continue but diminish in frequency: McCracken on 17 July, Sheares brothers and Oliver Bond on 26 July. Cornwallis adopts more humane approach: Amnesty Act passed 20 July and agreement with Newgate prisoners follows. French still active: Napoleon reaches Alexandria on 2 July and wins Battle of the Pyramids on 21 July but loses Battle of the Nile on 1 August; Humbert sails from La Rochelle for Ireland that day.

Wednesday, 22 August Humbert lands at Killala, Co. Mayo, and takes possession of town.

Thursday, 23 August Lake and Cornwallis learn

of landing. Humbert gets supplies ashore and United Irishmen begin to join him.

Friday, 24 August Humbert consolidates position in Killala. Lake and Cornwallis leave Dublin for West.

Saturday, 25 August Humbert attacks and takes Ballina. Lake and Cornwallis still travelling westward.

Sunday, 26 August Humbert leaves Ballina and marches to attack Castlebar overnight. Lake reaches Castlebar by midnight.

Monday, 27 August Humbert storms and seizes Castlebar; Lake and government forces retreat to Tuam; rebel units take Westport and Newport. Napper Tandy leaves French coast for Ireland in corvette.

Tuesday, 28 August Cornwallis reaches Athlone. Lake at Tuam and Humbert at Castlebar maintain defensive postures.

Wednesday, 29 August Humbert remains in Castlebar for third day. Cornwallis joins main government force at Tuam.

Thursday-Monday, 30 August-3 September Stalemate: Humbert entrenched at Castlebar, Lake and Cornwallis at Tuam. Humbert makes John Moore 'President of Connaught'.

Tuesday, 4 September Lake and Cornwallis move army to within twelve miles of Castlebar. Humbert leads troops off to northwest during evening in response; marches through night into Co. Sligo. United Irishmen begin to mobilise in Longford and Westmeath.

Wednesday, 5 September Humbert defeats small government force at Collooney, near Sligo town; reaches Drumahair, Co. Leitrim, by nightfall. Small government force seizes Castlebar; Lake follows Humbert; Cornwallis marches back towards Athlone. United Irishmen in Longford and Westmeath create large camps near Mullingar and Granard.

Thursday, 6 September Humbert moves from Drumahair to Drumkeeran. Rebel force in Longford devastated in attempted attack on Granard.

Friday, 7 September Humbert crosses Shannon at Ballintra and reaches Cloone, Co. Leitrim, by nightfall; Lake follows him across. Westmeath rebels destroyed in sudden attack by government forces near Mullingar.

Saturday, 8 September Humbert surrounded at Ballinamuck, Co. Longford, and surrenders after brief battle.

Sunday-Tuesday, 9-11 September Executions of captured rebels. French force taken towards Dublin. Only Killala and Ballina in French/rebel hands.

Wednesday, 12 September Ballina rebels launch unsuccessful attack on Castlebar.

Thursday-Saturday, 13-15 September Stalemate: rebels still hold Killala and Ballina; government forces at Castlebar, reinforcements under Trench on the way to strengthen them.

Sunday, 16 September Flotilla under Bompard, with Wolfe Tone aboard, sails from Brest.

Monday, 17 September Napper Tandy lands at Rutland, Co. Donegal. Passes night on land.

Tuesday, 18 September Tandy departs and sails away to France via North Atlantic and North Sea.

Wednesday-Friday, 19-21 September Stalemate continues in Mayo.

Saturday, 22 September Col Trench leads army out of Castlebar to move on rebel holdouts in northern Mayo.

Sunday, 23 September Trench sweeps into and takes Ballina in morning; attacks and overwhelms rebel force at Killala in afternoon.

Friday, 12 October Bompard's fleet reaches Lough Swilly and is captured.

Thursday, 8 November Tone taken to Dublin.

Saturday, 10 November Tone tried and condemned to death.

Monday, 12 November Tone cuts own throat.

Monday, 19 November Tone dies in prison from wound.

INDEX

D

1998 YEARBOOK

Incorporating

The 1798 Bicentennial Commemorative Events

Key to Yearbook Symbols

★ 1998 Bicentennial Commemorative Event

⚔ 1798 Historical event

1997

	JANUARY					FEBRUARY					MARCH					APRIL			
Sunday	-	5	12	19	26	-	2	9	16	23	30	2	9	16	23	-	6	13	20
Monday	-	6	13	20	27	-	3	10	17	24	31	3	10	17	24	-	7	14	21
Tuesday	-	7	14	21	28	-	4	11	18	25	-	4	11	18	25	1	8	15	22
Wednesday	1	8	15	22	29	-	5	12	19	26	-	5	12	19	26	2	9	16	23
Thursday	2	9	16	23	30	-	6	13	20	27	-	6	13	20	27	3	10	17	24
Friday	3	10	17	24	31	-	7	14	21	28	-	7	14	21	28	4	11	18	25
Saturday	4	11	18	25	-	1	8	15	22	-	1	8	15	22	29	5	12	19	26

	MAY					JUNE					JULY					AUGUST			
Sunday	-	4	11	18	25	1	8	15	22	29	-	6	13	20	27	31	3	10	17
Monday	-	5	12	19	26	2	9	16	23	30	-	7	14	21	28	-	4	11	18
Tuesday	-	6	13	20	27	3	10	17	24	-	1	8	15	22	29	-	5	12	19
Wednesday	-	7	14	21	28	4	11	18	25	-	2	9	16	23	30	-	6	13	20
Thursday	1	8	15	22	29	5	12	19	26	-	3	10	17	24	31	-	7	14	21
Friday	2	9	16	23	30	6	13	20	27	-	4	11	18	25	-	1	8	15	22
Saturday	3	10	17	24	31	7	14	21	28	-	5	12	19	26	-	2	9	16	23

	SEPTEMBER					OCTOBER					NOVEMBER					DECEMBER			
Sunday	-	7	14	21	28	-	5	12	19	26	30	2	9	16	23	-	7	14	21
Monday	1	8	15	22	29	-	6	13	20	27	-	3	10	17	24	1	8	15	22
Tuesday	2	9	16	23	30	-	7	14	21	28	-	4	11	18	25	2	9	16	23
Wednesday	3	10	17	24	-	1	8	15	22	29	-	5	12	19	26	3	10	17	24
Thursday	4	11	18	25	-	2	9	16	23	30	-	6	13	20	27	4	11	18	25
Friday	5	12	19	26	-	3	10	17	24	31	-	7	14	21	28	5	12	19	26
Saturday	6	13	20	27	-	4	11	18	25	-	1	8	15	22	29	6	13	20	27

1998

	JANUARY					FEBRUARY					MARCH					APRIL			
Sunday	-	4	11	18	25	1	8	15	22	-	1	8	15	22	29	-	5	12	19
Monday	-	5	12	19	26	2	9	16	23	-	2	9	16	23	30	-	6	13	20
Tuesday	-	6	13	20	27	3	10	17	24	-	3	10	17	24	31	-	7	14	21
Wednesday	-	7	14	21	28	4	11	18	25	-	4	11	18	25	-	1	8	15	22
Thursday	1	8	15	22	29	5	12	19	26	-	5	12	19	26	-	2	9	16	23
Friday	2	9	16	23	30	6	13	20	27	-	6	13	20	27	-	3	10	17	24
Saturday	3	10	17	24	31	7	14	21	28	-	7	14	21	28	-	4	11	18	25

	MAY					JUNE					JULY					AUGUST			
Sunday	31	3	10	17	24	-	7	14	21	28	-	5	12	19	26	30	2	9	16
Monday	-	4	11	18	25	1	8	15	22	29	-	6	13	20	27	31	3	10	17
Tuesday	-	5	12	19	26	2	9	16	23	30	-	7	14	21	28	-	4	11	18
Wednesday	-	6	13	20	27	3	10	17	24	-	1	8	15	22	29	-	5	12	19
Thursday	-	7	14	21	28	4	11	18	25	-	2	9	16	23	30	-	6	13	20
Friday	1	8	15	22	29	5	12	19	26	-	3	10	17	24	31	-	7	14	21
Saturday	2	9	16	23	30	6	13	20	27	-	4	11	18	25	-	1	8	15	22

	SEPTEMBER					OCTOBER					NOVEMBER					DECEMBER			
Sunday	-	6	13	20	27	-	4	11	18	25	1	8	15	22	29	-	6	13	20
Monday	-	7	14	21	28	-	5	12	19	26	2	9	16	23	30	-	7	14	21
Tuesday	1	8	15	22	29	-	6	13	20	27	3	10	17	24	-	1	8	15	22
Wednesday	2	9	16	23	30	-	7	14	21	28	4	11	18	25	-	2	9	16	23
Thursday	3	10	17	24	-	1	8	15	22	29	5	12	19	26	-	3	10	17	24
Friday	4	11	18	25	-	2	9	16	23	30	6	13	20	27	-	4	11	18	25
Saturday	5	12	19	26	-	3	10	17	24	31	7	14	21	28	-	5	12	19	26

1999

	JANUARY					FEBRUARY					MARCH					APRIL			
Sunday	31	3	10	17	24	-	7	14	21	28	-	7	14	21	28	-	4	11	18
Monday	-	4	11	18	25	1	8	15	22	-	1	8	15	22	29	-	5	12	19
Tuesday	-	5	12	19	26	2	9	16	23	-	2	9	16	23	30	-	6	13	20
Wednesday	-	6	13	20	27	3	10	17	24	-	3	10	17	24	31	-	7	14	21
Thursday	-	7	14	21	28	4	11	18	25	-	4	11	18	25	-	1	8	15	22
Friday	1	8	15	22	29	5	12	19	26	-	5	12	19	26	-	2	9	16	23
Saturday	2	9	16	23	30	6	13	20	27	-	6	13	20	27	-	3	10	17	24

	MAY					JUNE					JULY					AUGUST			
Sunday	30	2	9	16	23	-	6	13	20	27	-	4	11	18	25	1	8	15	22
Monday	31	3	10	17	24	-	7	14	21	28	-	5	12	19	26	2	9	16	23
Tuesday	-	4	11	18	25	1	8	15	22	29	-	6	13	20	27	3	10	17	24
Wednesday	-	5	12	19	26	2	9	16	23	30	-	7	14	21	28	4	11	18	25
Thursday	-	6	13	20	27	3	10	17	24	-	1	8	15	22	29	5	12	19	26
Friday	-	7	14	21	28	4	11	18	25	-	2	9	16	23	30	6	13	20	27
Saturday	1	8	15	22	29	5	12	19	26	-	3	10	17	24	31	7	14	21	28

	SEPTEMBER					OCTOBER					NOVEMBER					DECEMBER			
Sunday	-	5	12	19	26	31	3	10	17	24	-	7	14	21	28	-	5	12	19
Monday	-	6	13	20	27	-	4	11	18	25	1	8	15	22	29	-	6	13	20
Tuesday	-	7	14	21	28	-	5	12	19	26	2	9	16	23	30	-	7	14	21
Wednesday	1	8	15	22	29	-	6	13	20	27	3	10	17	24	-	1	8	15	22
Thursday	2	9	16	23	30	-	7	14	21	28	4	11	18	25	-	2	9	16	23
Friday	3	10	17	24	-	1	8	15	22	29	5	12	19	26	-	3	10	17	24
Saturday	4	11	18	25	-	2	9	16	23	30	6	13	20	27	-	4	11	18	25

HOLIDAYS AND NOTABLE DATES 1998

REPUBLIC OF IRELAND

v Year's Day	January 1
Patrick's Day	March 17
od Friday Bank Holiday	April 10
ster Monday	April 13
y Day	May 4
e Holiday	June 1
gust Holiday	August 3
tober Holiday	October 26
istmas Day	December 25
Stephen's Day Holiday	December 28

SCOTLAND

w Year's Day	January 1
iday	January 2
od Friday Bank Holiday	April 10
ing Holiday	May 4
y Day Holiday	May 25
mmer Holiday	August 3
istmas Day	December 25
xing Day Holiday	December 28

DATES TO REMEMBER 1998

Valentine's Day	February 14
rove Tuesday	February 24
ther's Day	March 22
mmer Time begins	March 29
her's Day	June 14
mmer Time ends	October 25
membrance Sunday	November 8

RELIGIOUS CALENDAR 1998

phany	January 6
n Wednesday	February 25
st Sunday in Lent	March 1
m Sunday	April 5
od Friday	April 10
ster Day	April 12
cension Thursday	May 21
it Sunday/Pentecost	May 31
Trinity Sunday	June 7
Corpus Christi	June 11
All Saints	November 1
Christmas Day	December 25

ENGLAND AND WALES

New Year's Day	January 1
Good Friday	April 10
Easter Monday	April 13
May Day Holiday	May 4
Spring Holiday	May 25
Summer Holiday	August 31
Christmas Day	December 25
Boxing Day Holiday	December 28

NORTHERN IRELAND

New Year's Day	January 1
St Patrick's Day Bank Holiday	March 17
Good Friday	April 10
Easter Monday	April 13
May Day Holiday	May 4
Spring Holiday	May 25
Holiday	July 13
Summer Holiday	August 31
Christmas Day	December 25
Boxing Day Holiday	December 28

JEWISH RELIGIOUS CALENDAR 1998

Passover, First Day of (Pesach)	April 11
Pentecost	May 31
New Year (5759) (Rosh Hashanah)	September 21
Day of Atonement (Yom Kippur)	September 30
Tabernacles, First Day of (Succoth)	October 5

MUSLIM RELIGIOUS CALENDAR 1998

Id-ul-Fitr	January 30
Id-ul-Adha	April 8
Islamic New Year (1419)	April 28
Ramadan, First Day of	December 20

INTERNATIONAL HOLIDAYS 1998

stria	Jan1, 6; Apr 13; May 1, 21; June 1; Aug 15; Oct 26; Nov 1; Dec 8, 25, 26
stralia	Jan 1, 26; Apr 10, 13, 25; June 12; Dec 25, 28
lgium	Jan 1; Apr 13; May 1, 21; June 1; July 21; Aug 15; Nov 1, 11, 15; Dec 25, 26
nada	Jan 1; Apr 10, 13; May 20; July 1; Sept 2; Oct 12; Nov 9; Dec 25, 26
nmark	Jan 1; Apr 9, 10, 13; May 3, 21; June 1, 5; Dec 25, 26
land	Jan 1, 6; Apr 10, 13; May 1, 21; June 1; July 14; Aug 1; Nov 1, 11; Dec 25
nce	Jan 1; Apr 13; May 1, 21; June 1; July 14; Aug 15; Nov 1, 11; Dec 25
rmany	Jan 1, 6; Apr 10, 13; May 1, 21; June 1, 11; Aug 15; Oct 3, 31; Nov 1, 18; Dec 25, 26
eece	Jan 1, 6; Mar 2, 25; Apr 17, 20; May 1; June 7; Aug 15; Oct 28; Dec 25, 26
y	Jan 1, 6; Apr 10; May 1; Aug 15; Nov 1; Dec 8, 25, 26
pan	Jan 1, 15; Feb 11; Mar 21; Apr 29; May 3, 5; Oct 10; Nov 3, 23; Dec 23
Luxembourg	Jan 1; Feb 23; Apr 13; May 1, 21; June 1, 23; Aug 15, 31; Nov 2; Dec 25, 26
Netherlands	Jan 1; Apr 10, 13, 30; May 1, 21; June 1; Dec 25, 26
New Zealand	Jan 1, 2; Feb 6; Apr 10, 13, 25; June 3; Oct 26; Dec 25, 28
Norway	Jan 1; Apr 9, 10, 13; May 1, 17, 21; June 1; Dec 25, 26
Portugal	Jan 1; Feb 24; Apr 10, 13, 25; June 10, 11; Aug 15; Oct 5; Nov 1; Dec 1, 8, 25
Spain	Jan 1, 6; Apr 10; May 1; Aug 15; Oct 12; Nov 1; Dec 6, 8, 25
Sweden	Jan 1; Apr 10, 13; May 1, 21; June 1, 22; Nov 7; Dec 25, 26
Switzerland	Jan 1, 2; Apr 10, 13; May 21; June 1; Aug 1; Dec 25, 26
USA	Jan 1, 19; Feb 16; May 25; July 4; Sept 7; Oct 12; Nov 11, 26; Dec 25

LAW SITTINGS 1998

Republic of Ireland		England and Wales		Northern Ireland		Scotland	
ary	Jan 12–Apr 3	*Hilary*	Jan 11–Apr 8	*Hilary*	Jan 6–Apr 3	*Hilary*	Jan 8–Apr 3
ster	Apr 20–May 28	*Easter*	Apr 21–May 22	*Trinity*	Apr 20–June 30	*Trinity*	Apr 21–July 3
nity	June 10–July 31	*Trinity*	June 2–July 31	*Michelmas*	Sept 5–Dec 21	*Michelmas*	Sept 15–Dec 12 (Provisional)
chelmas	Oct 5–Dec 21	*Michelmas*	Oct 1–Dec 21				

DECEMBER 1997
Nollaig 1997

Week 52.

DECEMBER					
S	M	T	W	T	F
	1	2	3	4	5
7	8	9	10	11	12
14	15	16	17	18	19
21	22	23	24	25	26
28	29	30	31		

Monday *Dé Luain* **22**

Tuesday *Dé Máirt* **23**

Wednesday *Dé Céadaoin* **24**

Thursday *Dé Déardaoin* **25**

Christmas Day. Bank & Public Holiday, Rep of Ireland, UK & USA

Friday *Dé hAoine* **26**

St Stephen's Day. Rep of Ireland/Boxing Day UK, Bank & Public Holiday, Rep of Ireland and UK

Saturday *Dé Sathairn* **27**

Sunday *Dé Domhnaigh* **28**

JANUARY					
M	T	W	T	F	S
			1	2	3
5	6	7	8	9	10
12	13	14	15	16	17
19	20	21	22	23	24
26	27	28	29	30	31

DECEMBER 1997/JANUARY 1998
Nollaig 1997/Eanáir 1998

Week 1. Days 1-4

onday *Dé Luain* **29**

esday *Dé Máirt* **30**

dnesday *Dé Céadaoin* **31**

★ '98 Opening Civic Ceremony – *Market Square, Enniscorthy, Co. Wexford*

ursday *Dé Déardaoin* **1**

v Year's Day, Bank & Public Holiday, Rep of Ireland, UK & USA

★ Ceremonial Flag Raising – *Enniscorthy, Co. Wexford, 12.00 noon*

day *Dé hAoine* **2**

day, Scotland

★ '98 Opening Concert – *opening commemoration featuring Anúna and guest artists from Wexford and beyond; The Cathedral, Enniscorthy, Co. Wexford*

turday *Dé Sathairn* **3**

Sunday *Dé Domhnaigh* **4**

JANUARY 1998
Eanáir 1998

Week 2. Days 5-11

			JANUARY			
S	M	T	W	T	F	S
				1	2	3
4	5	6	7	8	9	1C
11	12	13	14	15	16	17
18	19	20	21	22	23	24
25	26	27	28	29	30	31

Monday *Dé Luain* **5**

★ 'Women in '98' – *lecture series by Mary Cullen; ILAC Libra*
Dublin, 6.30p

Tuesday *Dé Máirt* **6**

Wednesday *Dé Céadaoin* **7**

★ 'Spies and Informers' – *lecture series by Prof Tom Bart*
(University College Dublin); Rathmines Libra
Dublin, 7

Thursday *Dé Déardaoin* **8**

Friday *Dé hAoine* **9**

Saturday *Dé Sathairn* **10**

Sunday *Dé Domhnaigh* **11**

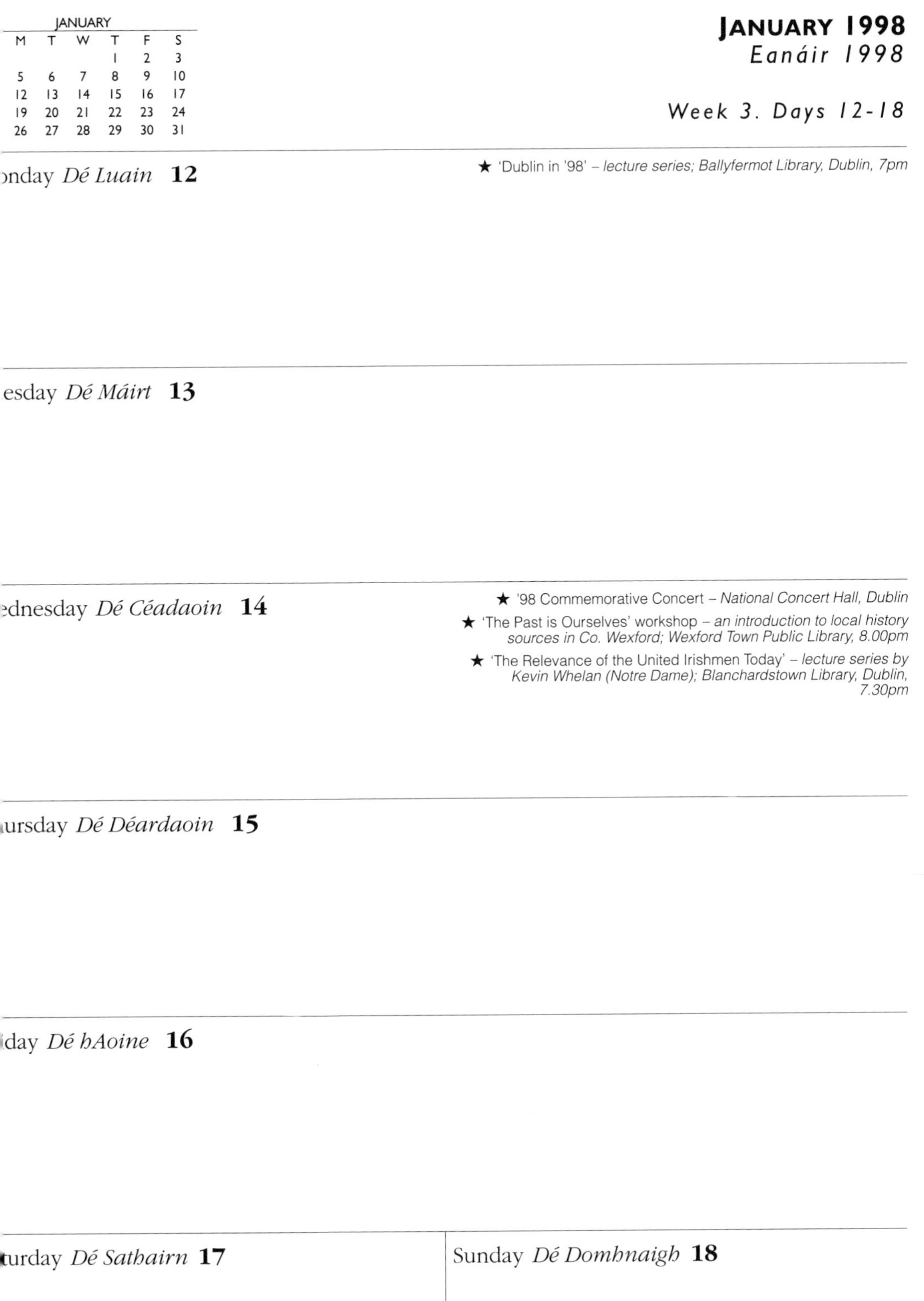

JANUARY					
M	T	W	T	F	S
			1	2	3
5	6	7	8	9	10
12	13	14	15	16	17
19	20	21	22	23	24
26	27	28	29	30	31

JANUARY 1998
Eanáir 1998

Week 3. Days 12-18

onday *Dé Luain* **12**

★ 'Dublin in '98' – *lecture series; Ballyfermot Library, Dublin, 7pm*

esday *Dé Máirt* **13**

ednesday *Dé Céadaoin* **14**

★ '98 Commemorative Concert – *National Concert Hall, Dublin*

★ 'The Past is Ourselves' workshop – *an introduction to local history sources in Co. Wexford; Wexford Town Public Library, 8.00pm*

★ 'The Relevance of the United Irishmen Today' – *lecture series by Kevin Whelan (Notre Dame); Blanchardstown Library, Dublin, 7.30pm*

ursday *Dé Déardaoin* **15**

iday *Dé hAoine* **16**

turday *Dé Sathairn* **17**

Sunday *Dé Domhnaigh* **18**

★ Christian Unity Week of Prayer – *Diocese of Ferns, Co. Wexford (until 25 January)*

JANUARY 1998
Eanáir 1998

Week 4. Days 19-25

JANUARY					
S	M	T	W	T	F
				1	2
4	5	6	7	8	9
11	12	13	14	15	16
18	19	20	21	22	23
25	26	27	28	29	30

Monday *Dé Luain* **19**

Holiday, USA

Tuesday *Dé Máirt* **20**

★ 'Women in '98' – *lecture series by Mary Cullen; Raheny Libr Dublin, 8*

Wednesday *Dé Céadaoin* **21**

Thursday *Dé Déardaoin* **22**

Friday *Dé hAoine* **23**

★ The John T Gilbert inaugural lecture: 'The Streets of Du Revisited' – *Mansion House, Dublin (invitation o*

Saturday *Dé Sathairn* **24**

Sunday *Dé Domhnaigh* **25**

★ 'The Origins of Uniting in Ulster' – *lecture series; Kilmainham Ja Dublin, 3pm*

onday *Dé Luain* **26**

stralia Day

esday *Dé Máirt* **27**

ednesday *Dé Céadaoin* **28**

★ 'The Literature of 1798 in County Wexford' workshop – *an introduction to sources; Wexford town Public Library, 8.00pm*

ursday *Dé Déardaoin* **29**

★ 'The Origins of Uniting in Ulster' – *lecture series; Donaghmede Library, Dublin, 6.45pm*

iday *Dé hAoine* **30**

turday *Dé Sathairn* **31**

Sunday *Dé Domhnaigh* **1**

★ Exhibition on 1798 – *bringing the story of 1798 to the widest possible audience, this exhibition includes state-of-the-art interactive and animated components; The National Library of Ireland, Dublin (until December 1998)*

★ 'Mightier than the Sword' – *a travelling exhibition celebrating local history publications; Wexford Public Libraries (until December)*

FEBRUARY 1998
Feabhra 1998

Week 6. Days 33-39

FEBRUARY					
S	M	T	W	T	F
1	2	3	4	5	6
8	9	10	11	12	13
15	16	17	18	19	20
22	23	24	25	26	27

Monday *Dé Luain* **2**

★ 'Catholic Priests in '98' – *lecture series by Daire K*
(St Patrick's, Drumcondra); ILAC Library, Dublin, 6.3

Tuesday *Dé Máirt* **3**

★ 'The Past is Ourselves' workshop – *an introduction to local hi*
sources in Co. Wexford; New Ross Public Lib
Co. Wexford, 11.0

Wednesday *Dé Céadaoin* **4**

★ 'The Relevance of the United Irishmen Today' – *lecture serie*
Kevin Whelan (Notre Dame); Ballymun Library, Dublin, 6.4

Thursday *Dé Déardaoin* **5**

Friday *Dé hAoine* **6**

★ '98 Bridge Congress – *Talbot Hotel & Wexford Bridge C*
(to 8 Febru

Saturday *Dé Sathairn* **7**

★ Ballad Singing Festival – *The Wexford Traditional Singers Club host a relaxed and informal atmosphere, all singing unaccompanied; Hotel Rosslare, Rosslare Harbour, Co. Wexford (also 8 February)*

★ '98 seminar – *major speakers discuss issues to advance the understanding of the period of the rebellion; Ferrycarrig Hotel, Co. Wexford*

Sunday *Dé Domhnaigh* **8**

FEBRUARY					
M	T	W	T	F	S
2	3	4	5	6	7
9	10	11	12	13	14
16	17	18	19	20	21
23	24	25	26	27	28

nday *Dé Luain* **9**

esday *Dé Máirt* **10**

★ 'The Past is Ourselves' workshop – *an introduction to local history sources in Co. Wexford; Enniscorthy Public Library, 11.00am*

dnesday *Dé Céadaoin* **11**

★ 'Dublin in '98' – *lecture series; Swords Library, Co. Dublin, 7.30pm*

ursday *Dé Déardaoin* **12**

day *Dé hAoine* **13**

turday *Dé Sathairn* **14**
'alentine's Day

Sunday *Dé Domhnaigh* **15**

February 1998
Feabhra 1998

Week 8. Days 47-53

FEBRUARY						
S	M	T	W	T	F	
1	2	3	4	5	6	
8	9	10	11	12	13	
15	16	17	18	19	20	
22	23	24	25	26	27	

Monday *Dé Luain* **16**

Holiday, USA

Tuesday *Dé Máirt* **17**

★ 'The Literature of 1798 in County Wexford' workshop – *introduction to sources; New Ross Public Lib Co. Wexford, 11.0*

Wednesday *Dé Céadaoin* **18**

Thursday *Dé Déardaoin* **19**

⚒ *The Leinster Provincial Directory of the United Irishmen decl that it will not be diverted from its purpose by 'anything that coul done in parliam*

Friday *Dé hAoine* **20**

Saturday *Dé Sathairn* **21**

Sunday *Dé Domhnaigh* **22**

★ 'Women in '98' – *lecture series by Mary Cullen; Kilmainham Jai Dublin, 3pm*

MARCH					
M	T	W	T	F	S
2	3	4	5	6	7
9	10	11	12	13	14
16	17	18	19	20	21
23	24	25	26	27	28
30	31				

nday *Dé Luain* **23**

esday *Dé Máirt* **24**

★ 'The Literature of 1798 in County Wexford' workshop – *an introduction to sources; Enniscorthy Public Library, Co. Wexford, 11.00am*

dnesday *Dé Céadaoin* **25**

ırsday *Dé Déardaoin* **26**

★ 'The Road to '98 in Wexford' – *lecture series by Brian Cleary (Wexford); Deansgrange Library, Co. Dublin, 7pm*

lay *Dé hAoine* **27**

ırday *Dé Sathairn* **28**

Sunday *Dé Domhnaigh* **1**

First Sunday in Lent

St David's Day

★ Women's Month *at the Wexford Town Arts Centre*

★ National Inter-Club Cross-Country Championships – *inter-club championships at junior and senior level, featuring Ireland's best cross-country runners; Wexford Town Race Course*

March 1998
Márta 1998

Week 10. Days 61-67

MARCH					
S	M	T	W	T	F
1	2	3	4	5	6
8	9	10	11	12	13
15	16	17	18	19	20
22	23	24	25	26	27
29	30	31			

Monday *Dé Luain* **2**

★ 'The Wexford Republic' – *lecture series; ILAC Library, Du 6.3*

Tuesday *Dé Máirt* **3**

★ '98 The Show: Who Fears to Speak – *a blend of music, dra dance, film archive and still photography with added narration segmented journey through Wexford's history with an emphas '98; Dun Mhuire, Wexford town (until 9 Ma*

Wednesday *Dé Céadaoin* **4**

Thursday *Dé Déardaoin* **5**

★ '1798: Political or Sectarian' – *lecture series by Daire K (St Patrick's, Drumcondra); Tallaght Library, Dublin, 7.3*

Friday *Dé hAoine* **6**

Saturday *Dé Sathairn* **7**

Sunday *Dé Domhnaigh* **8**

M	T	W	T	F	S
MARCH					
2	3	4	5	6	7
9	10	11	12	13	14
16	17	18	19	20	21
23	24	25	26	27	28
30	31				

Week 11. Days 68-74

nday *Dé Luain* **9**

★ Open Ju-Jitsu Competition – *a competition featuring groups from all over Ireland; Newcastle Centre, Co. Down*

sday *Dé Máirt* **10**

dnesday *Dé Céadaoin* **11**

★ 'Michael Dwyer and Joseph Holt' – *lecture series by Ruan O'Donnell (St Patrick's, Drumcondra); Blanchardstown Library, Dublin, 7.30pm*

ırsday *Dé Déardaoin* **12**

⚒ *Members of the Leinster Directory of the United Irishmen, meeting in Dublin in the home of Oliver Bond, are arrested by government forces.*

lay *Dé hAoine* **13**

ırday *Dé Sathairn* **14**

Sunday *Dé Domhnaigh* **15**

★ Féis Charman – *an all-Irish event for children and teenagers with singing, recitation and instrumental competitions; Enniscorthy, Co. Wexford*

★ St Patrick's Weekend Festival *(until 17 March)*

MARCH					
S	M	T	W	T	F
1	2	3	4	5	6
8	9	10	11	12	13
15	16	17	18	19	20
22	23	24	25	26	27
29	30	31			

Monday *Dé Luain* **16**

★ 'Theobald Wolfe Tone' – *lecture series by Prof Tom B (University College Dublin); Ballyfermot L Dublin*

Tuesday *Dé Máirt* **17**

St Patrick's Day, Bank & Public Holiday, Rep of Ireland, Bank Holiday, N Ireland

Wednesday *Dé Céadaoin* **18**

★ 'Dublin in '98' – *lecture series; Rathmines Library, Dublin*

Thursday *Dé Déardaoin* **19**

Friday *Dé hAoine* **20**

Saturday *Dé Sathairn* **21**

Sunday *Dé Domhnaigh* **22**

Mother's Day

MARCH					
M	T	W	T	F	S
2	3	4	5	6	7
9	10	11	12	13	14
16	17	18	19	20	21
23	24	25	26	27	28
30	31				

nday *Dé Luain* **23**

esday *Dé Máirt* **24**

★ 'Michael Dwyer and Joseph Holt' – *lecture series by Ruan O'Donnell (St Patrick's, Drumcondra); Raheny Library, Dublin, 8pm*

dnesday *Dé Céadaoin* **25**

onal Day, Greece

ursday *Dé Déardaoin* **26**

★ 'The Origins of Uniting in Ulster' – *lecture series; Deansgrange Library, Co. Dublin, 7pm*

day *Dé hAoine* **27**

★ Set dancing workshop and céilí – *craic and ceol with the Kilmore Set Dancers; Kilmore Quay, Co. Wexford (until 28 March)*

urday *Dé Sathairn* **28**

Sunday *Dé Domhnaigh* **29**

Summer Time begins

★ 'The Road to '98 in Wexford' – *lecture series by Brian Cleary (Wexford); Kilmainham Jail, Dublin, 3pm*

March/April 1998
Márta/Aibreán 1998

Week 14. Days 89-95

MARCH						
S	M	T	W	T	F	
1	2	3	4	5	6	
8	9	10	11	12	13	1
15	16	17	18	19	20	2
22	23	24	25	26	27	2
29	30	31				

Monday *Dé Luain* **30**

★ Lecture on 1798 – *Down County Museum, Downpatrick, Co. Do*

⚒ *Government Viceroy, Lord Camden, issues a declaration, ' country is in a state of rebellion'. Effective martial*

Tuesday *Dé Máirt* **31**

Wednesday *Dé Céadaoin* **1**

★ Historian in Residence – *a programme of clinics, workshops research projects, based on the library local studies collection; Wexford Public Libraries (until end M*

★ '1798 in Co. Down' – *Down County Museum, Downpa Co. Down (until Decem*

★ 'Background to the 1798 Rising' – *an exhibition; Ballynahin Saintfield Libraries, Co. Down (until 2 J*

Thursday *Dé Déardaoin* **2**

★ 'Up in Arms: The 1798 Rebellion in Ireland' – *an exhibition; U Museum, Belfast (until Decem*

★ 'Women in '98' – *lecture series by Mary Cullen; Tallaght Lib Dublin, 7.3*

Friday *Dé hAoine* **3**

Saturday *Dé Sathairn* **4**

Sunday *Dé Domhnaigh* **5**

Palm Sunday

		APRIL			
M	T	W	T	F	S
		1	2	3	4
6	7	8	9	10	11
13	14	15	16	17	18
20	21	22	23	24	25
27	28	29	30		

APRIL 1998
Aibreán 1998

Week 15. Days 96-102

nday *Dé Luain* **6**

★ 'The Origins of Uniting in Ulster' – *lecture series; ILAC Library, Dublin, 8pm*

sday *Dé Máirt* **7**

★ Mozart Requiem '98 – *an international event with the Ulster Orchestra and soloists, choirs from Northern Ireland, the south-east and France. A remarkable cultural event commemorating all the dead of '98; Rowe Street Church, Wexford town*

lnesday *Dé Céadaoin* **8**

★ Mozart Requiem '98 – *National Concert Hall, Dublin*

★ '1798: Political or Sectarian' – *lecture series by Daire Keogh (St Patrick's, Drumcondra); Ballymun Library, Dublin, 6.45pm*

rsday *Dé Déardaoin* **9**

★ Mozart Requiem '98 – *St Anne's Cathedral, Belfast*

⚔ *The first meeting of the Grand Orange Lodge of Ireland takes place in the home of Thomas Verner, in Dublin.*

ay *Dé hAoine* **10**

Friday, Bank Holiday, Rep of Ireland, N Ireland & Scotland, Bank lic Holiday, England & Wales

rday *Dé Sathairn* **11**

Sunday *Dé Domhnaigh* **12**

Easter Sunday

APRIL 1998
Aibreán 1998

Week 16. Days 103-109

APRIL					
S	M	T	W	T	F
			1	2	3
5	6	7	8	9	10
12	13	14	15	16	17
19	20	21	22	23	24
26	27	28	29	30	

Monday *Dé Luain* **13**

Easter Monday, Bank & Public Holiday, Rep of Ireland & UK (ex Scotland) Bank Holiday, Scotland

★ Official Opening of Fr John Murphy Centre – *a reconstruction house Fr Murphy, one of the major figures of 1798, lived ir Centre depicts his life with 18th century memorabilia and arte Boolavogue, Co. We*

★ Celtic Golf Classic – *St Helen's Bay Golf Club, Co. We (until 15*

Tuesday *Dé Máirt* **14**

Wednesday *Dé Céadaoin* **15**

★ Slogadh '98 – *premier youth festival of Ireland with five d traditional and contemporary Irish song, dance, music and d Wexford town (until 19*

★ 'The Relevance of the United Irishmen Today' – *lecture seri Kevin Whelan (Notre Dame); Swords Library, Dublin, 7.*

Thursday *Dé Déardaoin* **16**

★ 'A Tale of Two Churches' – *Wexford (see local press for d*

Friday *Dé hAoine* **17**

Saturday *Dé Sathairn* **18**

Sunday *Dé Domhnaigh* **19**

onday *Dé Luain* **20**

esday *Dé Máirt* **21**

★ 'The Origins of Uniting in Ulster' – *lecture series; Raheny Library, Dublin, 8pm*

dnesday *Dé Céadaoin* **22**

★ All-Ireland Drama Festival – *Enniscorthy, Co. Wexford (until 2 May)*

ırsday *Dé Déardaoin* **23**

eorge's Day

⚔ *The disarming of counties Kildare, Laois, Offaly and Tipperary is underway.*

lay *Dé hAoine* **24**

★ Viking Festival – *entertainment for all the family with street theatre, fantastic costumes, games and music; Wexford town (until 4 May)*

ırday *Dé Sathairn* **25**

General Gerard Lake replaces Sir Ralph Abercromby as nmander-in-Chief of government forces in Ireland.

Sunday *Dé Domhnaigh* **26**

★ 'Dublin in '98' – *lecture series; Kilmainham Jail, Dublin, 3pm*

★ Unveiling of 1798 module – *the major events of 1798 in the Slieve Coillte area displayed in module form; Slieve Coillte, JF Kennedy Park, Co. Wexford*

★ Comhaltas Ceoltóirí Éireann Concert of Traditional Irish Music, Song and Dance – *Wexford town*

APRIL/MAY 1998
Aibreán/Bealtaine 1998

Week 18. Days 117-123

APRIL					
S	M	T	W	T	F
			1	2	3
5	6	7	8	9	10
12	13	14	15	16	17
19	20	21	22	23	24
26	27	28	29	30	

Monday *Dé Luain* **27**

The North Cork Militia arrive in Co. Wex
Martial law is declared th

Tuesday *Dé Máirt* **28**

Islamic New Year (1419)

Wednesday *Dé Céadaoin* **29**

Thursday *Dé Déardaoin* **30**

Queen's Day, Netherlands

★ 'Women in '98' – *lecture series by Mary Cullen; Deansgrange Lib*
Co. Dublin,

Friday *Dé hAoine* **1**

★ A Festival of France – *a celebration of contemporary French culture literature, cinema, art, language, cuisine; County Wexford Public Li Service (until Decem*

★ New Ross Watercolour Society Outdoor Art Exhibit
New Ross, Co. Wexford (until

★ Unveiling of Harvey/Colclough memorial plac
Kilmore Quay, Co. We

★ 'Dublin and the Men of '98' – *an exhibition; Dublin Corporation P Libraries (until Decem*

Saturday *Dé Sathairn* **2**

★ GAIN All-Ireland Inter-schools Showjumping Championships – *County Showgrounds, Enniscorthy, Co. Wexford*

★ Caim Commemoration – *wreathlaying at Reynell's Tomb, Monart, Co. Wexford*

Sunday *Dé Dombnaigh* **3**

onday *Dé Luain* **4**

★ 'Theobald Wolfe Tone' – *lecture series by Prof Tom Bartlett (University College Dublin); ILAC Library, Dublin, 6.30pm*

y Day Holiday, Rep of Ireland & UK (ex Scotland),
ing Holiday, Scotland

esday *Dé Máirt* **5**

ednesday *Dé Céadaoin* **6**

★ Art exhibition: a Tony O'Malley retrospective – *New Ross Public Library, Co. Wexford (until 22 May)*

ursday *Dé Déardaoin* **7**

★ 'Michael Dwyer and Joseph Holt' – *lecture series by Ruan O'Donnell (St Patrick's, Drumcondra); Tallaght Library, Dublin, 7.30pm*

iday *Dé hAoine* **8**

turday *Dé Sathairn* **9**

Federation of Local History Societies – *a spring seminar involving cal history societies on a national level combining lectures and sits; Talbot Hotel, Wexford town*

Sunday *Dé Domhnaigh* **10**

★ Bank of Ireland Comóradh Cup Soccer Final

★ Fleadh Cheoil Charman – *Ferns, Co. Wexford*

★ Portable Art '98 – *an exhibition of the best of contemporary Irish art on the theme of '98; The Watch House Gallery, Enniscorthy, Co. Wexford (until 18 July)*

May 1998
Bealtaine 1998

Week 20. Days 131-137

			MAY			
S	M	T	W	T	F	S
31					1	2
3	4	5	6	7	8	9
10	11	12	13	14	15	16
17	18	19	20	21	22	23
24	25	26	27	28	29	30

Monday *Dé Luain* **11**

★ 'The Road to '98 in Wexford' – *lectures series by Brian Cle (Wexford); Ballyfermot Library, Dublin, 7*

Tuesday *Dé Máirt* **12**

Wednesday *Dé Céadaoin* **13**

★ Castledockrell Commemoration – *Castledock Enniscorthy, Co. Wexf*

The disarming continues and spreads to Co. Wickl

Thursday *Dé Déardaoin* **14**

★ 'Catholic Priests in '98' – *lecture series by Daire Keogh (St Patric Drumcondra); Donaghmede Library, Dublin, 6.45*

Friday *Dé hAoine* **15**

Saturday *Dé Sathairn* **16**

★ Open Boat Competition – *deep sea angling; Kilmore Quay, Co. Wexford (until 17 May)*

★ Telecom All-Ireland Football Championships – *Pairc Charman, Wexford town (until 17 May)*

Sunday *Dé Domhnaigh* **17**

MAY					
M	T	W	T	F	S
				1	2
4	5	6	7	8	9
11	12	13	14	15	16
18	19	20	21	22	23
25	26	27	28	29	30

MAY 1998
Bealtaine 1998

Week 21. Days 138-144

nday *Dé Luain* 18

⚒ *The new National Directory of the United Irishmen meets in Dublin. The date for the rebellion is set.*

esday *Dé Máirt* 19

★ '1798 in Print' – *an exhibition highlighting contemporary accounts of the events of 1798, from the Wexford County Library's Local Studies Collection; Wexford Town Public Library (until 23 May)*

★ 'Dublin in '98' – *lecture series; Raheny Library, Dublin, 8pm*

⚒ *Lord Edward Fitzgerald is arrested in Dublin.*

dnesday *Dé Céadaoin* 20

★ '1798, A Bicentenary Perspective' – *an International Academic Conference investigating 1798 from an international, national and local perspective; Ulster Museum, Belfast & Dublin Castle (until 24 May)*

ırsday *Dé Déardaoin* 21

⚒ *The brothers John & Henry Sheares are arrested.*

lay *Dé hAoine* 22

★ Boolavogue '98 Weekend – *early summer festival incorporating Boolavogue, The Harrow and Oulart – all important '98 locations. A weekend with something for all the family – open-air village concert, exhibitions, displays, recitals; Boolavogue, Co. Wexford (until 24 May)*

★ French/Irish Music & Food Festival – *Collooney, Co. Sligo (until 24 May)*

ırday *Dé Sathairn* 23

Concert – *a concert to commemorate the original date of the ıg; Smithfield, Dublin City Centre*

AIMS Choral Festival – *a music-filled weekend featuring choral ıps from all over. High standard competitive singing; New Ross, Wexford (until 24 May)*

John T Gilbert and his World' – *a travelling exhibition; Dublin poration Public Libraries (until 30 June)*

The rebellion begins in Leinster, chiefly in Co. Kildare. The rgents are repulsed at Naas and Clane, are defeated at ıangan, but are victorious at the Battle of Prosperous. In Co. ford, Anthony Perry is arrested, tortured and forced to name the ciple United Irish leaders in the area. John Colclough and vard Fitzgerald (Newpark) are arrested and imprisoned.

Sunday *Dé Domhnaigh* 24

★ Oulart Commemoration – *Oulart, Co. Wexford*

★ 'The Relevance of the United Irishmen Today' – *lecture series by Kevin Whelan (Notre Dame); Kilmainham Jail, Dublin, 3pm*

⚒ *Rebellion spreads. In Dublin, the insurgents are defeated at Lucan, Lusk, Rathfarnham and Tallaght. In Kildare the insurgents are defeated at Kilcullen Bridge, Monasterevin and Naas but are successful at Old Kilcullen and Rathangan. The insurgents are victorious at Barretstown, Co. Kilkenny; they are victorious at Dunboyne, Co. Meath, but are defeated at Slane. In Co. Wicklow, the insurgents are defeated at Baltinglass.*

⚒ *Thirty-four suspected United Irish prisoners shot in Dunlavin, Co. Wicklow.*

May 1998
Bealtaine 1998

Week 22. Days 145-151

MAY					
S	M	T	W	T	F
31					1
3	4	5	6	7	8
10	11	12	13	14	15
17	18	19	20	21	22
24	25	26	27	28	29

Monday *Dé Luain* **25**

⚔ *Twenty-four United Irish prisoners shot at Carnew, Co. Wick*

Tuesday *Dé Máirt* **26**

⚔ *The insurgents are defeated at Tara – this marks the end o rebellion in Co. Meath. Rebellion begins in Co. Wexford. Fr John Mu & local people confront the Camolin yeomanry at The Harrow. Tho Bookey, Lieutenant of the yeomanry, is k*

Wednesday *Dé Céadaoin* **27**

⚔ *Government troops sack Ballitore, Co. Kildare. Insurgents, le Fr John Murphy, Edward Roche and Morgan Byrne defeat the North Militia at Oulart Hill. The militia destroy a chapel and hous Boolavo*

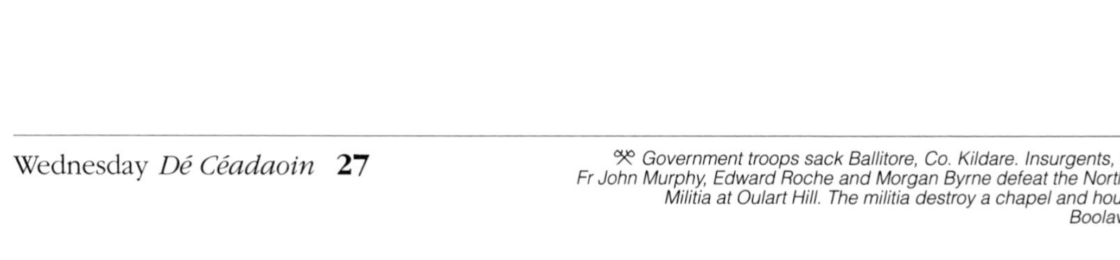

Thursday *Dé Déardaoin* **28**

⚔ *In the first Battle of Enniscorthy, the insurgents take the*

Friday *Dé hAoine* **29**

★ The inaugural meeting of the reconvention of the Wexford Se Weekend – *Johnstown Castle, Wexford (until 31*

★ Wexford Open Tennis Weekend – *Wexford Harbour Boat & T Club (until 1*

⚔ *The Insurgents camp on Vinegar Hill, outside Enniscorthy town Ulster Directory of the United Irishmen meets to plan rebellion in cou Antrim and Down. More than three hundred insurgent prisoner executed at the Curragh, Co. Kild*

Saturday *Dé Sathairn* **30**

★ International Horse-Driven Carriage Event – *Ballynahinch, Co. Down.*

★ Three Rocks Commemoration – *Barntown, outside Wexford town*

⚔ *Before dawn the Wexford insurgents are victorious at the Battle of Three Rocks. The insurgents take Wexford town, and liberate prisoners including Bagenal Harvey. A Committee of Public Safety is established.*

Sunday *Dé Domhnaigh* **31**

★ Commemoration at Carrigbyrne Hill – *the reopening of historic Evoy's Forge is at the centre of this commemoration. Carrigbyrne H was the site of the rebel camp; Carrigbyrne Hill, Co. Wexford*

★ RECONVENTION OF THE WEXFORD SENATE AT JOHNSTOWN CASTLE

⚔ *Bagenal Harvey is appointed as commander of the insurgent forces. Establishment of civilian government in Wexford town led by four Protestants and four Catholics.*

JUNE					
M	T	W	T	F	S
1	2	3	4	5	6
8	9	10	11	12	13
15	16	17	18	19	20
22	23	24	25	26	27
29	30				

JUNE 1998
Meitheamh 1998

Week 23. Days 152-158

nday *Dé Luain* 1

Holiday, Rep of Ireland

★ Wexford's Folk Memories – *an exhibition of stories, photographs and costumes celebrating Wexford's rich folklore; County Museum, Enniscorthy, Co. Wexford (until November)*

★ Comóradh Mini World Cup – *countywide in Wexford (until end July)*

★ The work of Mick O'Dea and Liz Rackard – *an art exhibition; New Ross Public Library, Co. Wexford (until end June)*

★ Commemoration of Battle of Newtownbarry – *pageant of 1798, festival of peace, fringe events; Bunclody, Co. Wexford*

⚔ *The insurgents are defeated at Bunclody, and at Ballymenane Hill, Gorey, Co. Wexford.*

esday *Dé Máirt* 2

⚔ *The insurgents are defeated at Kilcock, Co. Kildare (also 3 June)*

dnesday *Dé Céadaoin* 3

ursday *Dé Déardaoin* 4

★ The Gathering of the Bantry Men – *a pageant, Monksgrange House, Killanne, Co. Wexford*

⚔ *The insurgents defeat government troops at the Battle of Tubberneering, Co. Wexford, and occupy Gorey. In Dublin, Lord Edward Fitzgerald dies.*

day *Dé hAoine* 5

★ 'The Battle of Ballynahinch' – *an exhibition; Ballynahinch Public Library, Co. Down (until 30 September)*

★ Memorial Wreathlaying – *Scullabogue, Co. Wexford*

★ Representing the Battle of Ross – *a pageant; New Ross, Co. Wexford and surrounding district.*

★ Fair Days Festival – *New Ross, Co. Wexford*

★ World Sheepshearing Championships – *Rugby Club, Gorey, Co. Wexford*

⚔ *The military abandon Carnew, Co. Wicklow. The insurgents fail to capture New Ross, Co. Wexford; John Kelly of Killanne is wounded seriously. Over one hundred Catholic and Protestant loyalist prisoners are massacred at Scullabogue, Co. Wexford. Fr Philip Roche is chosen to replace Bagenal Harvey as commander of the insurgent army.*

Constitutional Day, Denmark

urday *Dé Sathairn* 6

onal Day, Sweden

Sunday *Dé Domhnaigh* 7

Trinity Sunday

★ Piercestown / Murrintown Commemoration – *Johnstown Castle was the house of Cornelius Grogan, rebel leader; Rathaspeck /Johnstown Castle, near Wexford town*

⚔ *In Ulster, Henry Joy McCracken leads insurgent forces in an unsuccessful attack on Antrim town.*

JUNE 1998
Meitheamh 1998

Week 24. Days 159-165

JUNE					
S	M	T	W	T	F
	1	2	3	4	5
7	8	9	10	11	12
14	15	16	17	18	19
21	22	23	24	25	26
28	29	30			

Monday *Dé Luain* **8**

⚔ *The rebellion breaks out in Co. Down, led by Henry Munro. Ir Wexford, insurgents capture the mailboat near Duncar*

Tuesday *Dé Máirt* **9**

★ Lecture/debate on the 1798 Rising – *Ballynahinch Library, Co. D*

★ 'Representations of 1798' – *an exhibition and workshop progra based on the County Library Local Studies Collection; Wexford Public Library (until 31 Au*

⚔ *The insurgents are defeated at the Battle of Arklow, Co. Wicklo Michael Murphy is killed in ac*

Wednesday *Dé Céadaoin* **10**

National Day, Portugal

⚔ *Pike Sunday, Co. Down – the insurgents are repulsed at Porta Co. Down. Five hundred insurgents capture Maynooth, Co. Kil*

Thursday *Dé Déardaoin* **11**

Friday *Dé hAoine* **12**

★ 'The Legacy of 1798' – *a conference; Down County Muse Downpatrick, Co. Down (until 14 J*

⚔ *The insurgents attack Borris House, Co. Carlow, and are repul*

Saturday *Dé Sathairn* **13**

★ International Ballad Writing Competition Finals – *Kilmore Quay, Co. Wexford*

⚔ *Munro and the insurgents are defeated at the Battle of Ballinahinch, Co. Down – the rebellion in Ulster is over.*

Sunday *Dé Domhnaigh* **14**

Father's Day

★ Flower Festival – *Collooney & Ballisodare, Co. Sligo (until 27 June)*

★ National Ecumenical Service – *St. Patrick's Cathedral, Dublin, 3.15pm*

★ Lacken Hill Pageant – *a pageant commemorating the events at Lacken Hill rebel camp 200 years ago; Lacken Hill, nr. New Ross, C Wexford*

JUNE					
M	T	W	T	F	S
1	2	3	4	5	6
8	9	10	11	12	13
15	16	17	18	19	20
22	23	24	25	26	27
29	30				

JUNE 1998
Meitheamh 1998

Week 25. Days 166-172

nday *Dé Luain* **15**

esday *Dé Máirt* **16**

⚒ *Engagement at Mountpleasant, nr. Tinahely, Co. Wicklow. Henry Munro is executed in Lisburn, Co. Down.*

dnesday *Dé Céadaoin* **17**

⚒ *The insurgents burn Tinahely, Co. Wicklow.*

ursday *Dé Déardaoin* **18**

★ Floral Harmony – County Flower Show, Ferns, Co. Wexford

⚒ *The Kildare insurgents are routed at Ovidstown, near Kilcock, Co. Kildare. Inconclusive skirmishing at Kilcavan Hill, Co. Wexford, is followed by retreat of the insurgent force towards Gorey, Co. Wexford.*

day *Dé hAoine* **19**

★ Commemoration of the Battle of Goff's Bridge – *this battle went on through the night of 19 June and into the day of 20 June; Foulkesmills, Co. Wexford (until 20 June)*

⚒ *Fr Philip Roche and the insurgents are forced to retreat from Lacken Hill to Three Rocks, near Wexford Town.*

urday *Dé Sathairn* **20**

Thomas Dixon and his followers massacre loyalist prisoners on xford town bridge. Fr Philip Roche and the insurgents are eated at Goff's Bridge and Foulkesmills by Sir John Moore's es.

Sunday *Dé Domhnaigh* **21**

★ VINEGAR HILL DAY – *THE LARGEST INTERNATIONAL OUTDOOR EVENT OF THE COMMEMORATIVE YEAR; ENNISCORTHY, CO. WEXFORD*

★ Unveiling of memorial at Duncormick, Co. Wexford

⚒ *Government forces recapture Enniscorthy and Wexford town; the insurgents, having been routed at Vinegar Hill, retreat southwards.*

JUNE 1998
Meitheamh 1998

Week 26. Days 173-179

JUNE					
S	M	T	W	T	F
	1	2	3	4	5
7	8	9	10	11	12
14	15	16	17	18	19
21	22	23	24	25	26
28	29	30			

Monday *Dé Luain* **22**

★ From Sleedagh to Tomduff, Co. Wexford – *a 52-mile spons walk retracing the epic march by Fr John Murphy after the r defeat at the Battle of Vinega*

⚒ *Fr John Murphy and the insurgents march towards Kilke*

Tuesday *Dé Máirt* **23**

National Day, Luxembourg

⚒ *The insurgents defeat government troops at Goresbri Co Kilke*

Wednesday *Dé Céadaoin* **24**

★ Byrne-Perry Summer School – *Gorey, Co. Wex (until 26 J*

⚒ *The insurgents take Castlecomer, Co. Kilke*

Thursday *Dé Déardaoin* **25**

⚒ *Fr Philip Roche, Matthew Keogh and other insurgents are har on Wexford Town Bridge. The insurgents capture Hacketst Co. Carlow (also 26 J*

Friday *Dé hAoine* **26**

★ Ballindaggin Commemoration – *Co. Wex*

★ Féile na nGael – *national festival of under-14 hurling, camog handball; countywide in Co. Wexford (until 28 J*

⚒ *Fr John Murphy and the insurgents are defeate Kilcumney Hill, Co. Ca*

Saturday *Dé Sathairn* **27**

★ Strawberry Fair – *nine days of fun, music and craic to celebrate the annual strawberry harvest. Free street entertainment, exhibitions, music, strawberries and cream and much more; Enniscorthy, Co. Wexford (until 5 July)*

★ County Wexford Agricultural Show – *Enniscorthy, Co. Wexford (until 28 June)*

⚒ *Cornelius Grogan and Bagenal Harvey are tried in Wexford town and sentenced to death.*

Sunday *Dé Domhnaigh* **28**

★ Bagenal Harvey Flotilla – *to commemorate Bagenal Harvey's retreat, Wexford Harbour to the Saltee Islands*

⚒ *John Colclough is tried and sentenced to death. Colclough, Grogan and Harvey are executed on Wexford town bridge.*

day *Dé Luain* 29

★ Tullow Commemoration – *Fr John Murphy of Boolavogue was executed at Tullow; Tullow, Co. Carlow (until 5 July)*

sday *Dé Máirt* 30

⚔ *Insurgents ambush and annihiliate the Ancient Britons at Ballyellis, Co. Wexford.*

nesday *Dé Céadaoin* 1

★ Summer Fun in Wexford – *young people's arts events and workshops in music, dance, drama, theatre, film, painting, crafts and more besides; in thirty venues countywide (until end August)*
Canada Day

rsday *Dé Déardaoin* 2

⚔ *Fr John Murphy and James Gallagher are executed at Tullow, Co. Carlow. The insurgents scatter yeomen at Ballyraheene Hill, near Shillelagh, Co. Wicklow.*

ay *Dé hAoine* 3

rday *Dé Sathairn* 4

endence Day

damstown Agricultural Show – *Adamstown, Co. Wexford*

exford insurgents are dislodged from White Heap mountain and the Battle of Ballygullen ends inconclusively – this marks nd of the rebellion in Co. Wexford (also 5 July)

Sunday *Dé Domhnaigh* 5

★ Eileen Aroon Festival – *lively summer family festival at the foot of Mount Leinster. Competitions, sports, music, quiz nights and open air music; The Square, Bunclody, Co. Wexford (until 19 July)*

JULY					
S	M	T	W	T	F
			1	2	3
5	6	7	8	9	10
12	13	14	15	16	17
19	20	21	22	23	24
26	27	28	29	30	31

Monday *Dé Luain* **6**

Tuesday *Dé Máirt* **7**

★ The work of Stephen Rothschild and Kathleen Delaney – *exhibition; New Ross Public Library, Co. Wexford (until 2*

Wednesday *Dé Céadaoin* **8**

Thursday *Dé Déardaoin* **9**

★ Wexford Town in Bloom – *a festival for all town residents and v (until 1*

★ Bannow & Rathangan Show – *horses, ponies, cattle, sheep, donkeys, horse & pony jumping, side saddle, flowers, industries, photography, dog show, horticulture; Killag, Dunco Co. W*

Friday *Dé hAoine* **10**

★ Seafood Festival – *Kilmore Quay, Co. W (until 1*

⚔ *The Co. Wexford insurgents skirmish at Kill, on their way forces with the insurgents of Co. K*

Saturday *Dé Sathairn* **11**

★ Tour de France in Ireland – *stages in the largest annual sporting event in the world; Dublin city*

⚔ *Insurgents attack and fail to take Clonard, Co. Meath.*

Sunday *Dé Domhnaigh* **12**

★ Tour de France in Ireland – *Dublin & North Wicklow*

★ Children's Festival & Family Events – *Teeling Centre, Colloon Co. Sligo (until 18 July)*

★ Rebels! in The Year of Liberty, 1798 – *a musical tribute to 17 by Danny Doyle and the TYL, St Michael's Theatre, New Ross, C Wexford*

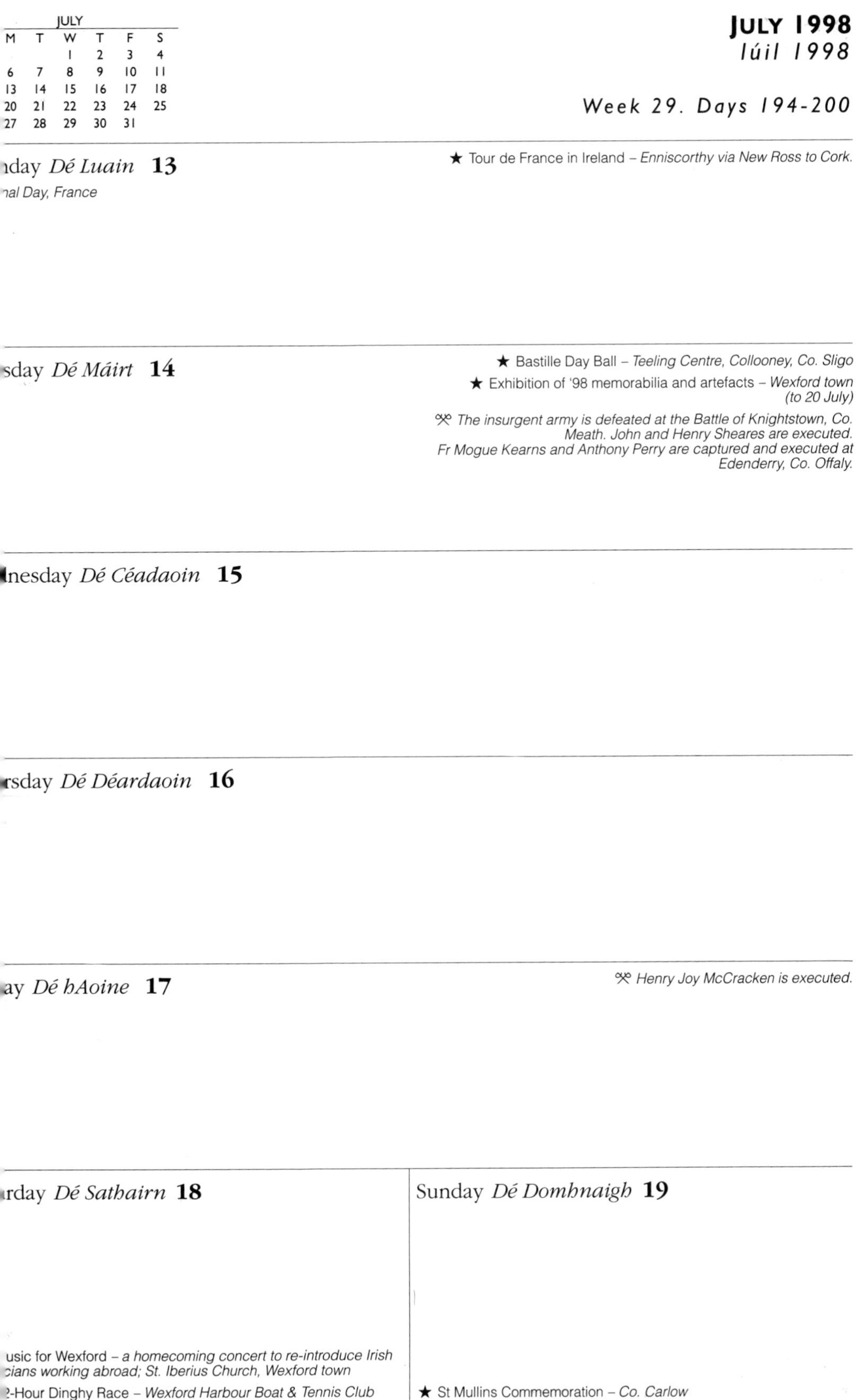

			JULY			
M	T	W	T	F	S	
		1	2	3	4	
6	7	8	9	10	11	
13	14	15	16	17	18	
20	21	22	23	24	25	
27	28	29	30	31		

JULY 1998
Iúil 1998

Week 29. Days 194-200

---

nday *Dé Luain* **13**

nal Day, France

★ Tour de France in Ireland – *Enniscorthy via New Ross to Cork.*

---

sday *Dé Máirt* **14**

★ Bastille Day Ball – *Teeling Centre, Collooney, Co. Sligo*

★ Exhibition of '98 memorabilia and artefacts – *Wexford town (to 20 July)*

⚔ *The insurgent army is defeated at the Battle of Knightstown, Co. Meath. John and Henry Sheares are executed. Fr Mogue Kearns and Anthony Perry are captured and executed at Edenderry, Co. Offaly.*

---

nesday *Dé Céadaoin* **15**

---

rsday *Dé Déardaoin* **16**

---

ay *Dé hAoine* **17**

⚔ *Henry Joy McCracken is executed.*

---

rday *Dé Sathairn* **18**

usic for Wexford – *a homecoming concert to re-introduce Irish cians working abroad; St. Iberius Church, Wexford town*

2-Hour Dinghy Race – *Wexford Harbour Boat & Tennis Club*

Sunday *Dé Domhnaigh* **19**

★ St Mullins Commemoration – *Co. Carlow*

July 1998
Iúil 1998

Week 30. Days 201-207

JULY					
S	M	T	W	T	F
			1	2	3
5	6	7	8	9	10
12	13	14	15	16	17
19	20	21	22	23	24
26	27	28	29	30	31

Monday *Dé Luain* **20**

Tuesday *Dé Máirt* **21**

Independence Day, Belgium

★ Phil Murphy Festival – *traditional arts festival with the best of r song, dance and storytelling; Carrig-on-Bannow, Co. We (until 26*

Wednesday *Dé Céadaoin* **22**

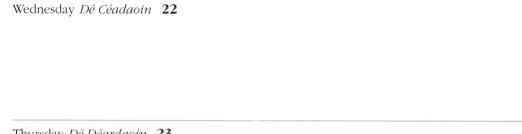

Thursday *Dé Déardaoin* **23**

Friday *Dé hAoine* **24**

Saturday *Dé Sathairn* **25**

★ Music for Wexford – *a homecoming concert to re-introduce Irish musicians working abroad; St Iberius Church, Wexford town*

Sunday *Dé Domhnaigh* **26**

★ Killanne Commemoration – *an ecumenical blessing of the 17 memorial at the cross of Killanne; Co. Wexford*

★ Irish Tug-of-War Association Championships – *Enniscorthy, Co. Wexford*

AUGUST					
M	T	W	T	F	S
31					1
3	4	5	6	7	8
10	11	12	13	14	15
17	18	19	20	21	22
24	25	26	27	28	29

nday *Dé Luain* **27**

sday *Dé Máirt* **28**

lnesday *Dé Céadaoin* **29**

rsday *Dé Déardaoin* **30**

ay *Dé hAoine* **31**

★ Summer Fair – *an annual event with something for all the family with great music and entertainment in the streets of this lovely town, exhibitions, competitions, historical tours and much more; Gorey, Co. Wexford (until 9 August)*

★ Open Tennis Weekend – *Boat Club, Wexford town (until 3 August)*

★ Riabhac – *a weekend of Celtic culture and craic with music, song, dance, language, crafts, storytelling, poetry and workshops; Enniscorthy, Co. Wexford (until 3 August)*

★ Kavanagh Clan Rally – *you don't have to be a Kavanagh to join in the celebrations! Ferns, Co. Wexford (until 3 August)*

rday *Dé Sathairn* **1**

ummer Fun in Wexford – *young people's arts events and shops in music, dance, drama, theatre, film, painting, crafts and besides; thirty venues countywide. Admission free end August)*

Sunday *Dé Domhnaigh* **2**

★ Campile Street Festival – *Co. Wexford*

AUGUST 1998
Lúnasa 1998

Week 32. Days 215-221

AUGUST					
S	M	T	W	T	F
30	31				
2	3	4	5	6	7
9	10	11	12	13	14
16	17	18	19	20	21
23	24	25	26	27	28

Monday *Dé Luain* **3**

Holiday, Rep of Ireland & Scotland

Tuesday *Dé Máirt* **4**

Wednesday *Dé Céadaoin* **5**

Thursday *Dé Déardaoin* **6**

⚔ *General Humbert sails from La Rochelle, France, with three fri*
and c.1,000

Friday *Dé hAoine* **7**

Saturday *Dé Sathairn* **8**

★ Music for Wexford – *a homecoming concert to re-introduce Irish musicians working abroad; St Iberius Church, Wexford town*

Sunday *Dé Domhnaigh* **9**

AUGUST					
M	T	W	T	F	S
31					1
3	4	5	6	7	8
10	11	12	13	14	15
17	18	19	20	21	22
24	25	26	27	28	29

AUGUST 1998
Lúnasa 1998

Week 33. Days 222-228

nday *Dé Luain* **10**

sday *Dé Máirt* **11**

nesday *Dé Céadaoin* **12**

rsday *Dé Déardaoin* **13**

ay *Dé hAoine* **14**

rday *Dé Sathairn* **15**

usic for Wexford – *a homecoming concert to re-introduce Irish cians working abroad; St Iberius Church, Wexford town*

aditional Music Festival – *Collooney, Co. Sligo 16 August)*

Sunday *Dé Domhnaigh* **16**

★ Steam Rally – *see steam power as it was used over 100 years ago; Tagoat, Co. Wexford*

AUGUST 1998
Lúnasa 1998

Week 34. Days 229-235

AUGUST					
S	M	T	W	T	F
30	31				
2	3	4	5	6	7
9	10	11	12	13	14
16	17	18	19	20	21
23	24	25	26	27	28

Monday *Dé Luain* **17**

Tuesday *Dé Máirt* **18**

Wednesday *Dé Céadaoin* **19**

★ 'Insurrection '98' – *historical documentary-drama depicting e during the turbulent time of 1798; Dun Mhuire, Wexford (until 29 Au*

★ General Humbert Summer School – *Ballina, Killala, La Co. Mayo (until 23 Au*

Thursday *Dé Déardaoin* **20**

Friday *Dé hAoine* **21**

Saturday *Dé Sathairn* **22**

★ Killala Festival – *a week-long festival consisting of pageant, fireworks, twinning ceremonies and honouring Killala's French connections; Killala, Co. Mayo (until 29 August)*

Sunday *Dé Domhnaigh* **23**

★ 1798 Humbert Commemoration & Walk – *Enniscoe /Laharda Crossmolina, Co. Mayo*

⚔ *The French army disembarks at Killala Bay, Co. Mayo.*

AUGUST					
M	T	W	T	F	S
31					1
3	4	5	6	7	8
10	11	12	13	14	15
17	18	19	20	21	22
24	25	26	27	28	29

AUGUST 1998
Lúnasa 1998

Week 35. Days 236-242

onday *Dé Luain* **24**

esday *Dé Máirt* **25**

The French and insurgents capture Ballina, Co. Mayo.

dnesday *Dé Céadaoin* **26**

ırsday *Dé Déardaoin* **27**

Humbert's Franco-Irish army defeats government forces at 'the Races of Castlebar', Co. Mayo.

lay *Dé hAoine* **28**

ırday *Dé Sathairn* **29**

einster Open Horseshoe Championships – *Enniscorthy, Wexford (until 30 August)*

98 Festival – *Ballinamuck, Co. Longford (until 5 September)*

Sunday *Dé Domhnaigh* **30**

AUGUST/SEPTEMBER 1998

Lúnasa/Meán Fómhair 1998

Week 36. Days 243-249

AUGUST

S	M	T	W	T	F
30	31				
2	3	4	5	6	7
9	10	11	12	13	14
16	17	18	19	20	21
23	24	25	26	27	28

Monday *Dé Luain* **31**

⚒ *Humbert proclaims the Provisional Republic of Conna*
Summer Holiday, UK (ex Scotland), Bank Holiday, Sco

Tuesday *Dé Máirt* **1**

Wednesday *Dé Céadaoin* **2**

Thursday *Dé Déardaoin* **3**

⚒ *Humbert evacuates Castlebar, which is then occupi*
government f

Friday *Dé hAoine* **4**

⚒ *Rebellion breaks out in the border areas of counties Longfor*
Westmeath. James Napper Tandy and a small French expedit
force sets sail from Dunkirk, France, for Ir

Saturday *Dé Sathairn* **5**

⚒ *Humbert's forces defeat the militia in a skirmish at Collooney, Co. Sligo. The insurgents occupy Wilson's Hospital, Multifarnham, Co. Westmeath. Government forces are victorious at Granard, Co. Longford.*

Sunday *Dé Domhnaigh* **6**

SEPTEMBER					
M	T	W	T	F	S
	1	2	3	4	5
7	8	9	10	11	12
14	15	16	17	18	19
21	22	23	24	25	26
28	29	30			

SEPTEMBER 1998
Meán Fómhair 1998

Week 37. Days 250-256

nday *Dé Luain* **7**

ay, USA

Humbert crosses the River Shannon into Co. Longford.

sday *Dé Máirt* **8**

★ 'Representations of 1798' – *an exhibition; Wexford Town Public Library (until 16 September)*

Following defeat at the Battle of Ballinamuck, Co. Longford, the French troops surrender. The Irish followers are massacred.

nesday *Dé Céadaoin* **9**

rsday *Dé Déardaoin* **10**

ay *Dé hAoine* **11**

★ Blackstairs Blues – *top-class worldwide jazz and blues performances, workshops, street busking, exhibitions; Enniscorthy, Co. Wexford (until 13 September)*

rday *Dé Sathairn* **12**

ne Battle of Carrignabat re-enacted – *Carrignabat, Co. Sligo*

he entire John T Gilbert' – *a conference; Dublin Corporation, Hall*

Sunday *Dé Domhnaigh* **13**

SEPTEMBER 1998
Meán Fómhair 1998

Week 38. Days 257-263

SEPTEMBER					
S	M	T	W	T	F
		1	2	3	4
6	7	8	9	10	11
13	14	15	16	17	18
20	21	22	23	24	25
27	28	29	30		

Monday *Dé Luain* **14**

Tuesday *Dé Máirt* **15**

Wednesday *Dé Céadaoin* **16**

⚒ *Napper Tandy disembarks from France at Rutland I.*
Co. Do

Thursday *Dé Déardaoin* **17**

⚒ *Nine French ships with c.3,000 men leave Brest, France, for Ir*
Wolfe Tone is in the com

Friday *Dé hAoine* **18**

Saturday *Dé Sathairn* **19**

Sunday *Dé Domhnaigh* **20**

SEPTEMBER					
M	T	W	T	F	S
	1	2	3	4	5
7	8	9	10	11	12
14	15	16	17	18	19
21	22	23	24	25	26
28	29	30			

nday *Dé Luain* **21**

⚒ *The insurgents are defeated at Grange, near Ballina, Co. Mayo.*
Jewish New Year (5759)

esday *Dé Máirt* **22**

⚒ *Government forces retake Ballina, Co. Mayo.*

dnesday *Dé Céadaoin* **23**

⚒ *Killala, Co. Mayo, is retaken by government forces – this marks the end of the rebellion in Connaught.*

ursday *Dé Déardaoin* **24**

★ RossDána – *poetry that moves, grooves and soothes – performance poetry at its best, with workshops to intrigue budding writers of all ages; New Ross, Co. Wexford (until 27 September)*

⚒ *Humbert's aide-de-camp, Bartholemew Teeling, is executed.*

day *Dé hAoine* **25**

★ Norman Connection Seminar – *Fethard-on-Sea, Co. Wexford (until 27 September)*

urday *Dé Sathairn* **26**

Sunday *Dé Domhnaigh* **27**

SEPTEMBER/OCTOBER 1998
Meán Fómhair/Deireadh Fómhair 1998

Week 40. Days 271-277

SEPTEMBER					
S	M	T	W	T	F
		1	2	3	4
6	7	8	9	10	11
13	14	15	16	17	18
20	21	22	23	24	25
27	28	29	30		

Monday *Dé Luain* **28**

Tuesday *Dé Máirt* **29**

★ National Ploughing Championships – *Ferns, Co. We*
(until 1 Octo

★ Comhaltas Ceoltóirí Éireann Concert of Traditional Music, So
Dance – *Ballina, Co. M*

Wednesday *Dé Céadaoin* **30**

Thursday *Dé Déardaoin* **1**

★ A Festival of France – *a celebration of contemporary French cu*
– literature, cinema, art, language, cuisine; County Wexford P
Library Service (until end Octo

Friday *Dé hAoine* **2**

★ Liberty, Equality & Fraternity – *a film festival; Wexford Film Cl*
Wexford Town Arts Centre (until 4 Octo

Saturday *Dé Sathairn* **3**

Day of Unity, Germany

Sunday *Dé Domhnaigh* **4**

OCTOBER					
M	T	W	T	F	S
			1	2	3
5	6	7	8	9	10
12	13	14	15	16	17
19	20	21	22	23	24
26	27	28	29	30	31

OCTOBER 1998

Deireadh Fómhair 1998

Week 41. Days 278-284

nday *Dé Luain* **5**

esday *Dé Máirt* **6**

dnesday *Dé Céadaoin* **7**

ursday *Dé Déardaoin* **8**

day *Dé hAoine* **9**

urday *Dé Sathairn* **10**

Sunday *Dé Domhnaigh* **11**

OCTOBER 1998
Deireadh Fómhair 1998

Week 42. Days 285-291

OCTOBER					
S	M	T	W	T	F
				1	2
4	5	6	7	8	9
11	12	13	14	15	16
18	19	20	21	22	23
25	26	27	28	29	30

Monday *Dé Luain* **12**

Holiday, USA, National Day, Spain

French ships are captured off the north-west coast; Wolfe To arrested and sent to D

Tuesday *Dé Máirt* **13**

Wednesday *Dé Céadaoin* **14**

Thursday *Dé Déardaoin* **15**

★ A Festival of African Literature – *County Wexford Public Lib (until 31 Oct*

★ Wexford Festival Opera – *three lesser-known operas of well-k composers and a wide programme of recitals, concert lectures. Fringe is lively; Theatre Royal and other venues in We town (until 1 Nover*

Friday *Dé hAoine* **16**

Saturday *Dé Sathairn* **17**

Sunday *Dé Domhnaigh* **18**

OCTOBER					
M	T	W	T	F	S
			1	2	3
5	6	7	8	9	10
12	13	14	15	16	17
19	20	21	22	23	24
26	27	28	29	30	31

OCTOBER 1998
Deireadh Fómhair 1998

Week 43. Days 292-298

nday *Dé Luain* **19**

esday *Dé Máirt* **20**

dnesday *Dé Céadaoin* **21**

ırsday *Dé Déardaoin* **22**

★ Antiques Fair – *the 1998 fair will include '98 memorabilia; Talbot Hotel, Wexford town (until 26 October)*

day *Dé hAoine* **23**

ırday *Dé Sathairn* **24**

Sunday *Dé Domhnaigh* **25**
Summer Time ends

OCTOBER/NOVEMBER 1998
Deireadh Fómhair/Samhain 1998

Week 44. Days 299-305

OCTOBER

S	M	T	W	T	F
				1	2
4	5	6	7	8	9
11	12	13	14	15	16
18	19	20	21	22	23
25	26	27	28	29	30

Monday *Dé Luain* **26**

October Holiday, Rep of Ireland, National Day, Austria

Tuesday *Dé Máirt* **27**

Wednesday *Dé Céadaoin* **28**

Thursday *Dé Déardaoin* **29**

Friday *Dé hAoine* **30**

Saturday *Dé Sathairn* **31**

Sunday *Dé Domhnaigh* **1**

★ Public Service: 100 Years of Wexford County Council – *an exhibition and workshop programme; Wexford Town Public Librar (until end November)*

		NOVEMBER			
M	T	W	T	F	S
2	3	4	5	6	7
9	10	11	12	13	14
16	17	18	19	20	21
23	24	25	26	27	28
30					

NOVEMBER 1998
Samhain 1998

Week 45. Days 306-312

onday *Dé Luain* **2**

uesday *Dé Máirt* **3**

ednesday *Dé Céadaoin* **4**

ursday *Dé Déardaoin* **5**

iday *Dé hAoine* **6**

turday *Dé Sathairn* **7**

Sunday *Dé Domhnaigh* **8**
Remembrance Sunday, UK

NOVEMBER 1998
Samhain 1998

Week 46. Days 313-319

NOVEMBER						
S	M	T	W	T	F	S
1	2	3	4	5	6	
8	9	10	11	12	13	
15	16	17	18	19	20	2
22	23	24	25	26	27	2
29	30					

Monday *Dé Luain* **9**

Tuesday *Dé Máirt* **10**

Wolfe Tone is tried and sentenced to de

Wednesday *Dé Céadaoin* **11**

Holiday, USA

Thursday *Dé Déardaoin* **12**

Wolfe Tone cuts his thr

Friday *Dé hAoine* **13**

Saturday *Dé Sathairn* **14**

Sunday *Dé Domhnaigh* **15**

NOVEMBER					
M	T	W	T	F	S
2	3	4	5	6	7
9	10	11	12	13	14
16	17	18	19	20	21
23	24	25	26	27	28
30					

NOVEMBER 1998
Samhain 1998

Week 47. Days 320-326

onday *Dé Luain* **16**

esday *Dé Máirt* **17**

ednesday *Dé Céadaoin* **18**

ursday *Dé Déardaoin* **19**

Wolfe Tone dies.

day *Dé hAoine* **20**

turday *Dé Sathairn* **21**

Sunday *Dé Domhnaigh* **22**

November 1998
Samhain 1998

Week 48. Days 327-333

NOVEMBER					
S	M	T	W	T	F
1	2	3	4	5	6
8	9	10	11	12	13
15	16	17	18	19	20
22	23	24	25	26	27
29	30				

Monday *Dé Luain* **23**

Tuesday *Dé Máirt* **24**

Wednesday *Dé Céadaoin* **25**

Thursday *Dé Déardaoin* **26**

Holiday, USA

Friday *Dé hAoine* **27**

Saturday *Dé Sathairn* **28**

Sunday *Dé Domhnaigh* **29**

First Sunday in Advent

DECEMBER

M	T	W	T	F	S
	1	2	3	4	5
7	8	9	10	11	12
14	15	16	17	18	19
21	22	23	24	25	26
28	29	30	31		

NOVEMBER/DECEMBER 1998
Samhain/Nollaig 1998

Week 49. Days 334-340

onday *Dé Luain* **30**
ndrew's Day

esday *Dé Máirt* **1**

dnesday *Dé Céadaoin* **2**

ursday *Dé Déardaoin* **3**

day *Dé hAoine* **4**

urday *Dé Sathairn* **5**

Sunday *Dé Domhnaigh* **6**
Independence Day, Finland

DECEMBER 1998
Nollaig 1998

Week 50. Days 341-347

DECEMBER					
S	M	T	W	T	F
		1	2	3	4
6	7	8	9	10	11
13	14	15	16	17	18
20	21	22	23	24	25
27	28	29	30	31	

Monday *Dé Luain* **7**

Tuesday *Dé Máirt* **8**

Wednesday *Dé Céadaoin* **9**

Thursday *Dé Déardaoin* **10**

Friday *Dé hAoine* **11**

Saturday *Dé Sathairn* **12**

Sunday *Dé Domhnaigh* **13**

onday *Dé Luain* **14**

esday *Dé Máirt* **15**

ednesday *Dé Céadaoin* **16**

ursday *Dé Déardaoin* **17**

iday *Dé hAoine* **18**

turday *Dé Sathairn* **19**

Sunday *Dé Domhnaigh* **20**

DECEMBER 1998
Nollaig 1998

Week 52. Days 355-361

DECEMBER					
S	M	T	W	T	F
		1	2	3	4
6	7	8	9	10	11
13	14	15	16	17	18
20	21	22	23	24	25
27	28	29	30	31	

Monday *Dé Luain* **21**

Tuesday *Dé Máirt* **22**

Wednesday *Dé Céadaoin* **23**

Thursday *Dé Déardaoin* **24**

Friday *Dé hAoine* **25**

Christmas Day, Bank & Public Holiday, Rep of Ireland, UK & USA

Saturday *Dé Sathairn* **26**

St Stephen's/Boxing Day

Sunday *Dé Domhnaigh* **27**

JANUARY					
M	T	W	T	F	S
				1	2
4	5	6	7	8	9
11	12	13	14	15	16
18	19	20	21	22	23
25	26	27	28	29	30

onday *Dé Luain* **28**

k & Public Holiday, Rep of Ireland & UK

esday *Dé Máirt* **29**

dnesday *Dé Céadaoin* **30**

ursday *Dé Déardaoin* **31**

day *Dé hAoine* **1**

Year's Day, Bank & Public Holiday, Rep of Ireland, UK & USA

urday *Dé Sathairn* **2**

Sunday *Dé Domhnaigh* **3**

YEAR PLANNER 1999 *(* = holidays)*

	JANUARY	FEBRUARY	MARCH	APRIL	MAY	JUNE
	** 1 Rep of Ireland & UK* ** 4 Scotland*		** 17 Rep of Irl & NI*	** 2 Rep of Irl & UK* ** 5 Rep of Irl & UK (ex. Scot)*	** 3 Rep of Irl & UK* ** 31 UK*	** 7 Rep of Irl*
Mon.		1	1			
Tue.		2	2			1
Wed.		3	3			2
Thu.		4	4	1		3
Fri.	1 *	5	5	2 *		4
Sat.	2	6	6	3	1	5
Sun.	3	7	7	4	2	6
Mon.	4 *	8	8	5 *	3 *	7 *
Tue.	5	9	9	6	4	8
Wed.	6	10	10	7	5	9
Thu.	7	11	11	8	6	10
Fri.	8	12	12	9	7	11
Sat.	9	13	13	10	8	12
Sun.	10	14	14	11	9	13
Mon.	11	15	15	12	10	14
Tue.	12	16	16	13	11	15
Wed.	13	17	17 *	14	12	16
Thu.	14	18	18	15	13	17
Fri.	15	19	19	16	14	18
Sat.	16	20	20	17	15	19
Sun.	17	21	21	18	16	20
Mon.	18	22	22	19	17	21
Tue.	19	23	23	20	18	22
Wed.	20	24	24	21	19	23
Thu.	21	25	25	22	20	24
Fri.	22	26	26	23	21	25
Sat.	23	27	27	24	22	26
Sun.	24	28	28	25	23	27
Mon.	25		29	26	24	28
Tue.	26		30	27	25	29
Wed.	27		31	28	26	30
Thu.	28			29	27	
Fri.	29			30	28	
Sat.	30				29	
Sun.	31				30	
Mon.					31 *	
Tue.						

* 12 N. Ireland
* 3 Rep of Irl & Scot
* 30 UK (ex Scot)
* 25 Rep of Irl
* 27 Rep of Irl & UK
* 28 Rep of Irl & UK

	JULY	AUGUST	SEPTEMBER	OCTOBER	NOVEMBER	DECEMBER
n.					1	
e.					2	
d.			1		3	1
u.	1		2		4	2
	2		3	1	5	3
t.	3		4	2	6	4
n.	4	1	5	3	7	5
n.	5	2	6	4	8	6
e.	6	3 *	7	5	9	7
d.	7	4	8	6	10	8
u.	8	5	9	7	11	9
	9	6	10	8	12	10
t.	10	7	11	9	13	11
n.	11	8	12	10	14	12
n.	12 *	9	13	11	15	13
e.	13	10	14	12	16	14
d.	14	11	15	13	17	15
u.	15	12	16	14	18	16
	16	13	17	15	19	17
t.	17	14	18	16	20	18
n.	18	15	19	17	21	19
n.	19	16	20	18	22	20
e.	20	17	21	19	23	21
d.	21	18	22	20	24	22
u.	22	19	23	21	25	23
	23	20	24	22	26	24
t.	24	21	25	23	27	25
n.	25	22	26	24	28	26
n.	26	23	27	25 *	29	27 *
e.	27	24	28	26	30	28 *
d.	28	25	29	27		29
u.	29	26	30	28		30
	30	27		29		31
t.	31	28		30		
n.		29		31		
n.		30				
e.		31				

ADDRESS/TEL.

ADDRESS/TEL.

Notes